Siaya

'The Luo of Kenya are a Nilotic people of some 500,000 souls bordering Lake Victoria Nyanza to the north and south of Kavirondo Gulf. Some outlying sections also stretch into Tanganyika. The parts of Luoland which lie back from the lake, e.g. Alego and Ugenya tribal areas, are undulating country in which the homesteads are built along the slopes. . . of the successive ridges. The country near the lake is less broken. The rainfall is everywhere heavy and well-distributed. The people are mainly agricultural, though they keep many cattle, sheep, and goats and most of their country is suitable for a pastoral life. Fishing plays a big part in the economy of the lakeside tribes. Hunting is little practiced today, but in the old days organized battues were a regular feature. The homestead, the residence of an elementary family or joint family, is generally called *dala*, a Bantu word, but in the more purely Luo parts of the country the Nilotic word *pacho* (pl. *mier*) is used, especially by the older men. It is usually surrounded by a thick hedge of euphorbia, a narrow gap in which is the entrance to the kraal, round which are the huts and granaries.'

E. E. Evans-Pritchard, 'Luo Tribes and Clans,'
Rhodes-Livingstone Journal 7 (1949), 24-5

Ogena to Ageno	She loves me, I love her
Rose Atieno lando	Rose Atieno the Brown.
An Achiedh Kure	What shall I do
Sani Koro ionge	Now that you're not there.
Atieno wananere	Atieno we shall meet,
Lady Nyar Alego	Lady from Alego.
Siaya ka baba	**Siaya, the home of our fathers.**
Kuro bende ionge	You are not there
Yenga ku midhiye	Yenga, where you went
Kuro bende ionge	You are not there
Mama!	Either!

"Song of Rose Atieno", by Juma Odundo, pop guitarist, 1967

In 1967, Siaya was created as a district headquarters ex nihilo *from a market. Most people of the region of Central Nyanza, now Siaya District, never thought it possible. It is Odundo's song which located Siaya in the consciousness of the people in advance of the actual construction of the present headquarters.*

EASTERN AFRICAN STUDIES

Abdul Sheriff
Slaves, Spices & Ivory in Zanzibar
Integration of an East African Commercial Empire
into the World Economy 1770-1873

Tabitha Kanogo
Squatters & the Roots of Mau Mau 1905-1963

David W. Throup
Economic and Social Origins of Mau Mau 1945-1953

Frank Furedi
*Mau Mau Betrayed**

David William Cohen & E.S. Atieno Odhiambo
Siaya
*the Historical Anthropology of an African Landscape**

Bruce Berman & John Lonsdale
Unhappy Valley
*Clan, Class & State in Colonial Kenya**

Siaya

The Historical Anthropology
of an African Landscape

DAVID WILLIAM COHEN
Professor of History & Anthropology
The Johns Hopkins University

E.S. ATIENO ODHIAMBO
Associate Professor in History
University of Nairobi

James Currey
LONDON
Heinemann Kenya
NAIROBI
Ohio University Press
ATHENS

James Currey Ltd
54b Thornhill Square
Islington
London N1 1BE, England

Heinemann Kenya
Kijabe Street, PO Box 45314
Nairobi, Kenya

Ohio University Press
Scott Quadrangle
Athens, Ohio 45701, USA

First published 1989

British Library Cataloguing in Publication Data
Cohen, David William, *1943-*
  Siaya: the historical anthropology of an
  African landscape.____ (Eastern African Studies).
  1. Kenya. Siaya. Cultural processes, to 1988
  I. Title   II. Odhiambo, E.S. Atieno, *1946-*
  III. Series
  306'.09676'2

ISBN 0-85255-034-0
ISBN 0-85255-035-9 Pbk

Library of Congress Cataloging-in-Publication Data
Cohen, David William.
  Siaya, the historical anthropology of an African landscape/David William
Cohen, E.S. Atieno Odhiambo.
    p. cm.
    Bibliography: p.
    Includes index.
    ISBN 0-8214-0901-8. ISBN 0-8214-0902-6 (pbk.)
    1. Luo (African people)   2. Land settlement patterns—Kenya—Siaya
District.   3. Rural-urban migration—Kenya—Siaya District.   4. Siaya
District (Kenya)—Social life and customs.   I. Atieno Odhiambo. E.S.,
1946-   II. Title.
DT433.545.L85C64 1988   88-15182
967.6'2—dc19   CIP

Typeset in 11pt Baskerville by Grassroots, London N3
Printed and bound in Great Britain

Contents

Maps

Illustrations

Colour photographs by David William Cohen 1979/1980

Acknowledgements

Many individuals and organizations have made possible this collaborative work and the research on which it is based. A National Science Foundation grant supported field research in Siaya between 1978 and 1982. The University of Nairobi and The Johns Hopkins University not only gave support to the research of each of us, but also made possible — in 1985-6 — an academic year together in the United States. We are particularly grateful to Dean George W. Fisher, Professors I. William Zartman, Michael Schatzberg, and John Russell-Wood of Johns Hopkins, and Professors Godfrey Muriuki and Ahmed I. Salim of the University of Nairobi for creating this opportunity for collaborative writing. Professor Franz Rottland of the University of Bayreuth and Professor Rudolf Vierhaus and Dr Hans Medick of the Max-Planck Institut für Geschichte in Göttingen made possible a further period of intensive work together in Germany in July 1986.

In numerous ways Professor B. A. Ogot encouraged this work and this collaboration and, with Grace Ogot, directed our attention to questions of the past of western Kenya that had not previously received sufficient attention from historians. Dr Ralph Herring and Dr John Lonsdale offered expert counsel concerning literature on the historical background of western Kenya. Dr John Onyango-Abuje made available his archaeological camp in Boro as a base for the research in the area of Boro and Lake Gangu. Elijah Oduor provided exceptional support, wise counsel, and skilful assistance through the field research at Boro. Michael Ochanda and Julius Oloo provided valuable assistance to the field research programme in Siaya.

Members of seminars and workshops in Baltimore, Bad Homburg, Bayreuth, Madison, Nairobi, New York, Paris, Stanford, and Washington, DC offered advice and criticism on sections of the manuscript. Jonathan Lewis, George Martin, Christopher Steiner and Carolyn Hamilton provided excellent assistance in Baltimore. The University of North Carolina Press has kindly permitted us to present in a slightly revised form a section of a chapter from Olivier Zunz (ed.), *Reliving the Past: The Worlds of Social History* (Chapel Hill, 1985). The second chapter appears in a similar form in *Cahiers d'Etudes Africaines*, no. 107-8, 1988.

Glossary

ajuoga: diviner
biero: placenta
chiemo: food
dala: home, enclosure
dalawa: patrimony
gorogoro: empty tin used as measure of volume
goyo dala: building a new home
goyo ligala: cutting a new foundation
gunda bur: ancient concentrated and fortified settlement
gweng: neighbourhood, region, country-side settlement
gwoma: 'loose girls'
jogam: 'go-betweens', negotiators for a prospective groom
jok: the powerful spirit-force
jokoyo: Luo 'untainted' by Western culture
joluo asili: 'typical' Luo persons
jomaranda: proper Luo, cultured persons
jonam: river-lake fishermen
jonanga: 'the people of clothes'
jooko: outsiders
jopango: migrant labourers
jopiny: Luo 'untainted' by Western culture
jopith: owners of the herd
jorieko: clever persons
josemb dhok: cattle guides
josomo: readers, the schooled
jowa: our people
juok: witchcraft
ka ojuok: within the euphorbia fence or the enclosure
karuoth: extended lineage group or clan of special status based on descent, a 'royal family'
kikapu (Swahili): basket
kuon jonanga: 'food of the clothed people'
kuon ongere: 'white man's food'

lam: light
langwa: our valiant ones
lowo: fertile soil
luth: travel insignia
magendo: smuggling
mbas: age-mates
migogo: married daughter
misumba: subordinates
mzungu: foreigner
ng'ato nono: outsider
nya: the process of spreading out
nyiego: rivalry between co-wives
oganda: broadest social unit recognizing a common history or descent, 'tribe'
okethore: spoilt, ruined
osiepe: friendship
pap: open field, pasture, particularly low-lying land
pim: elderly woman responsible for rearing young children and adolescents
piny: territory, country nation
posho (Swahili): food, ration
raia: ordinary folk
simba: the bachelor's house
siwindhe: the girls' house or dormitory in the enclosure
tajiri: the rich, wealthy
thur: homeground
thurwa: the past
timbe jonanga: 'ways of the clothed foreigners'
timbewa: culture
ugali: steamed maizemeal
uji (Swahili): porridge
wat: kinship
won piny: owner of the land
yawa: our agnates
yie: boat

Introduction

In just the last few years, ethnographers and anthropologists have raised serious questions about the possibility of understanding and representing other cultures and other societies.[1] The self-scrutiny and self-doubt that they are bringing to their craft portends the closing of a long era of confidence in the scientific practice of studying and describing other peoples. A generation of doubt may produce a broad reconstruction and revitalization of the social sciences; at worst, it may stifle new research.

The sciences of study of the 'other' developed out of the confident and earnest 'first' descriptions of other peoples produced by Western explorers, travellers, and missionaries. The claims to thoroughness and accuracy of these descriptions of the 'other' were nurtured because of the power that Europeans attributed to their own culture and to their own science. The power of Europeans in non-Western settings simply affirmed the power of European descriptions.

Work in the confident sciences of anthropology and ethnography rested upon two assumptions: first, that there were two distinct parties within the operation of the science of studying the 'other', the observer and the observed. 'One studies the Luba', but 'one does not write for the Luba'. Second, the discourse over the nature of the 'other' proceeds outside the 'other'. It develops within a sociology of practice and science particular to the West. The specific works of ethnography or anthropology were seen to develop within the structure of a Western scientific discipline and not from the way the 'observed' saw and represented themselves. Anthropological monographs and ethnographies were written for colleagues, students, and others brought up in a common intellectual tradition. They were not intended to make sense to those who had been 'observed', the subjects of study.

If, in the study of the 'other', we can now see an era of doubt supplanting an era of confidence, we must also recognize a fatal paradox inherent to each phase. As anthropologists saw their own task as certain and scientific, they could at the same time ignore, exclude from view, suppress, the evidence that 'other cultures' have been busy producing their own anthropologies and their own histories, discoursing on their own identities and constitutions, producing their own introspections.

On the other hand, as anthropology has come to be marked by intense self-scrutiny and self-doubt, the study of 'other cultures' has clearly ceased to be the monopoly of anthropology and of the earlier traveller literature parent to it. Historians in North America and Europe have developed powerful expertise in the study of societies and cultures in Asia, Latin America, and Africa. Political scientists, sociologists, linguists, and economists have all joined in the study of cultures outside Europe. Moreover, poetry, drama, film, and fiction — both about and from 'other cultures' — have become increasingly available to new audiences. Just as anthropologists and ethnographers are questioning the possibility of knowing the 'other', ordinary people across the globe are gaining images and knowledge of other cultures. The exchange of knowledge about 'other cultures' proceeds at an incredible pace, and substantially outside the academic disciplines that once monopolized such inquiry.

This book attempts to bring together the vision of the ethnographer and the vision of men and women within an 'other culture': the Luo of western Kenya. It is written both *about* and *for* the Luo. In it, Luo debates and Luo ideas about their own past and present are brought together with the findings, arguments, and questions produced about the Luo by scholars writing not for the Luo but for their own disciplines. It concentrates on a sequence of selected issues: the physical landscape and the reworking of the landscape over several centuries; the social impulses and intellectual processes producing broad collective identities; the multiple and overlapping settings of cultural activity; the sources and effects of food scarcity and the images and ideas to which it gives rise; the powers of women; and the ambiguities of education. With each of these subjects, we are concerned not simply with the ethnographic representation of the 'other'; indeed, it could be said that 'we go much less far' in this respect than a considerable number of outstanding scholars who have done research 'on the Luo'.

Here, we are primarily intrigued by the way in which these subjects are discussed, turned over, and debated among the Luo.[2] We sense that this dynamic edge of discourse is, first, older than the twentieth century; second, more than a product of modern schooling; and third, other than simply a response to the depictions of outside observers. After all, for the Luo, more than for the outside observers of the Luo, what constitutes culture, what is correct behaviour, what is history, are questions that are heavily fought over. And, crucially, these struggles constitute essential pieces of the past and of the present of Luo society and culture; they are intellectual debates that power the process and shape the structure of Luo culture and society.

Still, our intention is not to produce a 'Luo self-portrait' as opposition to an outsider's ethnography, any more than it is to impose an outsider's analysis upon the Luo. Rather, we attempt a perspective both removed and intimate: removed so that one can gain control of the sociology and intellectual history of the ethnographic literature itself; yet intimate so that one can come to terms with the ways in which people — in ordinary, commonplace activities — have produced society and culture not only through social practice but also through the formation of histories and anthropologies.

This book is an experiment (not least of which is its bi-national authorship), intended to be suggestive rather than exhaustive. We hope to show that this way of raising questions, of connecting disjointed yet revealing fragments of social life, of bringing together very different sorts of voices, helps readers to recognize the richness and complexity both of creating and of explaining culture.[3]

Since the publication of Bethwell Allan Ogot's *History of the Southern Luo* in 1967, no work has appeared that attempts to survey the literature on the past of the Luo-speaking peoples of western Kenya, whether presented as an appreciation of the field that Professor Ogot parented or as an inquiry into issues left open by these studies. This book takes up this challenge. It asks how one should set about understanding the Luo past and present. It begins by asking how best to define our unit of study. We have chosen to focus on one Luo-speaking district of western Kenya: Siaya. There are good grounds for doing so. Siaya, today a rural area involved in maize-growing, with small numbers of cattle associated with dispersed households, was the transit and settlement zone of the earliest Luo-speakers to enter what is today Kenya, some three and a half centuries ago. Groups and lineages that have maintained settlements in Siaya are the 'parents' of an expanding and dispersing Luo population. They spread east and south, across the Winam Gulf into South Nyanza and Tanzania, and more recently into the urban areas of East Africa. It is an ennobled landscape, for groups elsewhere refer in their histories to sacred or original sites in what is today Siaya.

When we speak of Siaya, therefore, part of our meaning is the formal administrative district of Siaya, with its population

3

of 474,516 people and its mappable boundaries.[4] But we also mean something more elusive yet more important than a territory: the way in which people in other places nevertheless identify with Siaya in the ways in which they construct their identities and organize their lives. The 1979 census records that Siaya has a 'net out-migration' of 133,717: that is, the difference between those born in the district and residing anywhere in Kenya and those residing in Siaya District proper. This is the highest out-migration figure for any district in Kenya and is also highest as a ratio of 'out-migrants' to district population. Indeed, slightly more than one-fifth of the Luo population of Kenya was enumerated outside Nyanza Province.[5] Luo residing in Nairobi represent 7.67 per cent of the total Luo population of Kenya.[6] It is perhaps with such figures in mind that social scientists, and also Luo, refer to Siaya as a classic example of a 'labour reserve'.

These realities can be and have been analysed in terms of migrations and wanderings; of tensions between custom and modernity. But the challenge is to understand their interrelations. Everyday life for the Luo outside Siaya is affected by connections with and images of Siaya; everyday life inside Siaya is affected by the fact of the diaspora. Our unit of study is this total field of interaction.

If this is the 'region' we are studying, how can we best approach its history? In recent years there has been a considerable development of academic historical literature about Siaya and western Kenya as a whole, mostly growing out of doctoral dissertation research. Like historical research elsewhere in Africa, its aim has been to *give* the people of western Kenya 'a history'. The authors of this book have themselves operated on this assumption. But we have come separately to realise the paradox of such an ambition. How can we talk of 'giving' a history to people who themselves constantly refer back to the past? We now try to reveal and make fertile this tension between our academic work and the knowledge and purposes of those we have chosen to study.

To explore these ambiguities of space and time — a multiple location and layers of historical activity — we have chosen a form of presentation that is open, suggestive, and, we hope, inviting to several different audiences: to historians, to social scientists more generally, *and* to the people of western Kenya.

The book is organized into six chapters. Chapter 1 takes up the changing forms of Luo settlement and residency and the changing ideas about these forms. Central to this discussion are the *gundni* (sing., *gunda*) *bur*: fortified and compact settlements, the remains of which can be seen today in Alego in the northern and western areas of Siaya. The contrast between the *gundni bur* of several centuries ago and the forms of recent and present settlements provides a context for discussing migration in the Luo past and the place of migration in the histories of that past. By looking at these histories and at Luo perceptions of settlement we challenge the dominant models of outside ethnography: the idea that the Luo form a 'classic, segmentary society'[7] and that their past largely consists of segmentary process.

Chapter 2 examines identity and its formation. It argues that a national Luo identity has been formed by complex social and ideological processes, rather than being the automatic result of segmentation. A notion of 'rehearsal' is introduced: the suggestion in the literature that earlier processes of formation of collective identities and groupings constitute a rehearsal of processes of formation of a regional or national identity in this century, that the 'Luo nation' is the Luo family writ large. Not only do we examine critically this notion; we also argue that Luo have used the broad Luo collectivities (*piny*) of this century as models for the historical reconstruction of pre-colonial organization. Once again the segmentary model is exposed as both a powerful and problematic model in the formation of a literature on the Luo past and Luo society. Expanded Luo identity has not simply been created by segmentary expansion from an original group of pioneer Luo. Instead, it has been built over time by actual actors in a process of dispute and contest.

Chapter 3 takes up the multiple characteristics of the unit of study and its many territories. It does this by presenting *several* Siaya landscapes: Kaloleni in Nairobi, Boro as part of Siaya District proper, southern Uganda, the new Sugar Belt in western Kenya. It explores the terms on which Siaya people have participated in the wider economy, and considers the pressures placed on Luo men to maintain good homes (*dala*) in the Siaya countryside, as places to be at home and to be buried, and as concrete acknowledgements of links to the past. The chapter examines patterns of accumulation, economic differentiation, and social stratification among the Luo.

Chapter 4 develops further the notion of a Siaya landscape as an economy marked above all by scarcity. The chapter opens with an incident of a child fainting from hunger, and the paralysis observed among a crowd of observers who had themselves experienced scarcity of food but did not recognize what to do in the case of a child collapsing from hunger. The discussion of hunger in the countryside leads into a consideration of the connections between the economy of scarcity in the household

5

in the countryside and the domestic setting of the migrant labourer. The remittance economy, on which most of the households of Siaya are critically dependent, is examined, as one encounters the considerable scope of women in the management of the rural household. Siaya is not generally recognized as one of those districts of Kenya — or, for that matter, as one of those regions of Africa — that experience extreme shortages of food and consequent hunger. Indeed, travellers in the nineteenth century reported that the region was remarkably abundant in surplus foodstuffs. A discussion of the paradox of abundance and the development of scarcity is presented. The chapter examines the cattle traders and the butchers as an example of transitional accumulators in the countryside in the twentieth century. The economy organized around the holding and exchange of cattle is viewed as a formed feature and not a given one, its context lying in the struggles to rebuild wealth after the epizootics of the late nineteenth century. The growth of the cattle economy and the development of the butcheries is seen in the context of an increasingly active and, from some perspectives, invasive state.

Chapter 5 takes up more closely the 'powers of women', which have been characterized in the earlier discussion of women managing rural households and estates as a consequence of the disappearance of fathers in Uganda, of the remittance economy, and of the deaths of husbands in road accidents. Additionally, some other situations are introduced: the role of women in medical therapy and psychotherapy; the historic, revered and now disappeared role of old women nurturing and educating young children and socializing them to a world wider than the household or enclosure, and the role of women in the founding and work of new churches. The much observed problem of children bearing children, and 'loose morals' generally, provides a context for discussing the relations between young men and women in the countryside and in the city. Marriage is represented through an analogy to marriage: the construction and launching of a Lake Victoria fishing vessel; and it is represented through a report of a negotiation of a marriage under not quite perfect circumstances. The discussion of women and marriage throws light on the ways in which Luo deal with their own observations of variance between norm and practice.

Finally Chapter 6 deals with learning, with the exchanges of knowledge through education and through gossip, and with the paradoxical situation of education, of schooling, as a not fully acknowledged status-according system in Siaya. The chapter brings forward knowledge from the shadows, knowledge of recent experience in Siaya, of a darker world, glimpsed and known, yet not broadly discussed. A story of a brief 'revolution' in Siaya is presented, with its ambiguous closure. The subject of friendship (*osiepe*) is raised into view and we see how meaning, value, and power are implicated in the ways in which friendship simultaneously fortifies and supplants kinship (*wat*) as a medium of organizing support. The consideration of friendship allows a further view, a reprise, of the changing shapes and force of kinship ideology in the lives of people of Siaya past and present.

The volume concludes with an Afterword, a brief presentation of the essence of a recent and much celebrated courtroom drama in which, between 20 December 1986 and 23 May 1987, parties fought over the rights to bury the remains of a well-known Kenyan lawyer, S.M. Otieno, reproducing within the court litigation many of the practices, tensions and ideas discussed throughout the book.

NOTES

1. For several important discussions of ethnography in crisis, see James Clifford and George E. Marcus (eds), *Writing Culture: The Poetics and Politics of Ethnography* (Berkeley, University of California Press, 1986) and Hans Medick, 'Missiǫnare im Ruderboot? Ethnologische Erkenntnisweisen als Herausforderung an die Sozialgeschichte', *Geschichte und Gesellschaft*, 10, 3 (1984), pp. 295-319.

2. The present authors depart from the argument of David Parkin, *The Cultural Definition of Political Response: Lineal Destiny among the Luo* (London, Academic Press, 1978), pp. 286-311, who suggests that the Luo of Kenya are marked and affected by the overarching condition of 'stifled cultural debate'. Our view is that this debate, the struggles over knowledge of past and over ordering culture and society are, and have been, exceedingly rich, and not necessarily resolved toward the models of past and present social organization that are conventionally and consensually held. Perhaps the difference here is one of relative measure of the intensity of the 'cultural debate'. But also, the present authors have taken into their view of this 'debate' the struggles for meaning, coherence, and authority within emerging Luo prose historiography, a subject that Parkin omits from his study of the Luo of Nairobi.

3. For an important example of this kind of scholarly enterprise, see T. O. Ranger, *Dance and Society in Eastern Africa, 1890-1970: The Beni Ngoma* (London, Heinemann, 1975).

4. The 1979 census gives the entire Luo population of Kenya as 1,955,845. This makes the Luo the third largest ethnic group ('tribe and nationality') in Kenya, falling behind the Luhya since the 1969 census. The Kikuyu rank first. The intercensal population increase figure (1969-79) for the Luo is 2.85 per cent, the second lowest rate of growth among 'major tribal groupings' in Kenya.

5. This is one of the highest figures for 'tribes and national groups' in Kenya. This figure does not, of course, include Luo of Kenya birth residing in Uganda, Tanzania, or overseas.

6. For the Kikuyu, the figure is only slightly higher: 8.64 per cent.

7. Parkin, *Cultural Definition*, offers the more refined expression 'polysegmentary lineage culture'.

Map 1: East Africa, Nyanza and Siaya

1. Damiano Ogutu's
   doorway, Uhanya
   1980

2. *Dala* at
   Damiano Ogutu's
   1980

3. 'The Market Place', Kisumu 1907
(from the John Ashworth gift to the Macmillan Library, Nairobi)

5. (opposite) On the road: Omoro Omolo (left) and Randiga Nundu (right) 1904
(from the Macmillan Library, Nairobi)

4. Enclosure c. 1920
(from the John Ainsworth gift to the Macmillan Library, Nairobi)

6(a). Enclosure 1979
6(b).Enclosure 1980

7. Farms on the land, near Boro 1980

8. Basket seller, Boro market 1979

9.*Kikapu* 1905
(from the Macmillan Library, Nairobi)

10. Young Men 1905
(from the Macmillan Library, Nairobi)

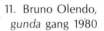

11. Bruno Olendo,
   gunda gang 1980

12. Othuogo Warina
of Kaleny-juok, Siaya 1980

Forms in the Siaya Landscape

For the person of Siaya, 'landscape' is not a reference to the physiognomy of the terrain. Rather, it evokes the possibilities and limitations of space: encompassing the physical land, the people on it, and the culture through which people work out the possibilities of the land. 'Landscape' means 'existence'.

'Land' is simultaneously and ambiguously *piny* (territory), *thur* (homeground), and *lowo* (reproductive soil). People — Luo people — are referred to as *jowa* (our people), *yawa* (our agnates), *langwa* (our valiant ones), *kothwa* (our seed). 'Culture' is referred to as *timbewa* (our way of doing things). A Siaya person thinks of home, *dala*, as a concept in which all these elements are interwoven into a fine seamless text; the texture of life in Boro, in

In among the thick hillside vegetation of the Sakwa area lie fields of maize and millet, and clusters of homesteads of thatched huts. Our village, like all Luo villages, was neatly fenced about by euphorbia trees or 'Ojuok' as we call them. Inside the circular village were twenty neatly built huts, forming a concentric circle within the fence. In the centre were four small huts which we regarded as the headquarters of the elders of the village. The one in the centre was the *duol* or office of the Jaduong Dala, or chief elder. He was Omuodo Alogo. Next to this hut was the office of Odinga, my father; then that of Oteke, the uncle of Omuodo Alogo; and the fourth belonged to a friend who had married one of our sisters and come to our village. Each hut in the village represented one woman. Elder Omuodo Alogo had six women, Odinga had five, Oteke had three, and so on. In all there were thirty-six children in the village.[1]

Ndigwa, in Dudi, which inevitably draws together into one meaningful assemblage the Asembo fisherman at Aram market, the urbane political economist from Seme in Cambridge, Massachusetts, and the stowaway Alego porter in Durban, South Africa. They all speak of one home, in Siaya, but the whole expanse of their experience is their 'landscape', from which they draw their material life, but also their poets, their oratory, and the threads with which they weave a meaningful interaction across space. Their very centre is the place where their umbilical cord is buried, *ka ojuok*, in the euphorbia fence which surrounds their homestead.

Older Luo often remark that before 1900 people did not go around building just anywhere on the terrain. The land was rationally organized, and people were settled in concentrated residential units (*gundni bur*; sing., *gunda bur*). Defensive requirements were important, according to these expositions, while collective settlements and collective planning of the use of the land were critical. In this popular exposition of agrarian change, devastation of the landscape came with the *pax Britannica*, when the defensive uses of the *gunda bur* became less significant.

According to this view, under the new order the desire of each person to have his own domain became explosive. There is the expression 'Even cowards want their own space'. There was a proliferation of homestead building and reallocations of functions of land. Soils once thought perfect for the growing of simsim (sesame) became Odongo's small estate, where he and members of his household planted maize and cassava. A millet field was similarly transformed into someone's enclosed space, where several different crops might be cultivated. According to this popular theory, the land quickly deteriorated; and the special resources and specialized production organized by larger social units were replaced by the monotonous repetition of small farms producing small amounts of basic staples. There is probably much truth in this presentation of rural transformation, though the period during which the *gunda bur* was being replaced by a new more atomized form of settlement probably lasted a century longer than this interpretation suggests, in many areas preceding the *pax Britannica*. An adjusted model would certainly include an intermediate stage during which people lived outside the old *gunda bur* but continued to work co-operatively across a much wider terrain, a pattern of production that the British encountered on their arrival, and labelled 'shifting cultivation'.

Curiously, this style of exposition overlooks the effect on the rhythm of production of coercive colonial taxes and labour demands, in which people in the countryside were forced to accept the logic of (not to say taste of) maize and cassava, over millet and sesame. The story is also quiet on the central place of labour availability in the organization of the Siaya farm, then and now. But the story of the transformation, as it is told in all its variant and consensual versions, alerts us to the fact that dynamic change is part of the way people in Siaya compose and tell history. Moreover, it indicates that they do not always present change as progress.

We know that at the latest by the nineteenth century a new pattern had been imposed upon the original principles of construction and occupation of the *gunda bur*. This involved sons leaving the *gunda bur* in turns — a process recalled as taking place in order of lineage seniority as opposed to uterine seniority — and building smaller homesteads close by. This act was and is referred to as *goyo dala* (building a home). And the rituals of establishment of new homes recall the establishment of the ancient settlements. The chicken, the axe, father and son, are elements in twentieth-century ritual that are held to be continuous with the foundation rituals of the ancestral *gunda bur* at Ligala in what is now the Kenya-Uganda borderland.

Land shortages in Siaya have recently introduced what appears to be a third phase of the transformation of the occupational landscape. This involves no actual movement from the paternal homestead. Rather, the sons are permitted to make a cutting in the ancestral fence and then build their main house facing an independent gate put together at the new breach. This has been a feature since the 1960s, and in common discussion it has come to be associated with Christian families. Christians in Siaya have found it easier to vary the protocol by stating that Christianity allows this variance on custom, though they cite no biblical source to support the proposition. The signposts of this new phase in the occupational landscape — producing essentially more — compressed settlements — are the homesteads of the Anglican Church 'padres'; the Musiga family (in Ugenya), the Nyong'o family (in Seme), the James Oganga family (in Alego).

Another transformation involves the way in which people speak of a homestead or compound. There is a shifting toponymy. In an important sense, language has followed reality; as women have emerged as primary occupants of Siaya compounds (with husbands, brothers, fathers far away as labour migrants), so there has been an increasing practice of people referring to compounds by the woman's name. For example, people say, 'I am going to Dorka Okinyo's home' as comfortably as they say 'I am going to Julius Abuje's home'.

The remoulding of authority in the Siaya rural household from man to woman has in this way begun a remodelling of the toponymic landscape of the countryside. It is a recognition of the long distance we have travelled from the *gunda bur* in the space of a century and a half. In this regard, 'Dorka's home', the woman's home, represents still further the diminution of collective activity and planning in the Siaya countryside, for the new toponym separates the conceptual form of the location from the idea that the home or compound is formed out of, is a physical representation of, the patrilineage.

Gunda bur

The neighbourhood of Gangu lies immediately north of Lake Gangu in western Siaya District. It is an area of about 2km by 3km. The historical literature on Luo settlement indicates that Gangu was a critical triangle, wedged between river and swamp, through which significant groups of early Luo, and others, passed.

At Gangu, seven trench and wall settlements, probably two to four centuries old, have been located, mapped, and diagrammed. These were *gundni bur*, ancient fortified settlements. By the late nineteenth century, it seems, these particular fort-ifications had been abandoned. Now we note only sections of trench and wall configurations passing across, or broken by, maize and cassava fields. These *gundni* were compact settlements, providing a modicum of security for sizable groups, stores of foodstuffs, and cattle. They stand in contrast to twentieth-century enclosures in the region, which are fenced and which constitute the residences of but small patri-groups.

Each village was a large defence fort. A wall of earth ten to fifteen feet high and about three feet in diameter went round the village leaving only one opening as the gate. The wall was surrounded by a ditch of seven to ten feet in depth. Inside the wall there were hundreds of huts in which lived large numbers of men, women and children. The land immediately around the homestead was reserved for cultivation by women and their daughters while the elders and male warriors grazed their flock in areas fur-ther away from the homestead.[2]

Through collections of oral material, it has been established that each of the seven settlements at Gangu experienced a sequence of occupation. The oral material is dense and somewhat difficult. Essentially, the researcher uncovers a sequence of 'micro-conquests', one following another fairly rapidly after the original construction of the trenches and walls. Some occupants enhanced the fortifications, others probably did not stay long enough to have the resources in labour to do so. The body of oral material is full of difficult nomenclature referring to conquering and occupying groups, and one of the early challenges of the work in Gangu was in establishing the identities of groups that constructed, captured, and used these fortified arrangements.[3]

The historical study of the *gunda bur* has involved going beyond the simple historical nomenclature and toward detailing the con-tent and significance of the identities of occupying groups. From reading the literature on Luo society, it was anticipated that these conquering and occupying groups would be lineages: groups most clearly defined as components of unilineal corporate groups established in the region. It was expected that the conquering and occupying groups would fit within the classic grammar of patrilineality and segmentation among the Nilotic Luo; for the people of Siaya speak of themselves as descended from ancient communities of Nilotic Luo-speakers in the southern Sudan.[4] These expectations were well founded. Historians of western Kenya have reconstructed migrational trends sufficient to underscore the popular view of a historic descent from the Upper Nile Valley and the Bahr el Ghazal in the Sudan.[5] Linguists have demonstrated the continuities in language.[6] Anthropologists have argued the identity of social institutions and cultural practices between peoples of western Kenya and peoples of the southern Sudan. Segmentation is held to be the primary and characteristic process of group formation among peoples of both regions and patrilineality is suggested as the prime mode of recruitment to groups and as the frame of interest articulation among individuals and households.[7]

Here in Gangu, one thought, it might be possible to detail, for a relatively remote past, the specific experiences of such segmentation within one narrow context. What was recovered, however, was something quite different. Examining the data for the serial occupations of these seven *gundni* of Gangu, one finds little indication of corporate action of agnatic groups, little evidence that segmentation was a prime process of group formation, or that patrilineality defined the modes of recruitment to the conquering groups. Rather, the conscious accounts of settlement where those are available, and the reconstruction of one *gunda*, Gangu, indicate that conquering and occupying groups were constructed through alliances of unrelated individuals and alliances marked by affinal connections.

Ivor Wilks has implicated a similar process of social combination in his discussion of possible linkages between the formation of powerful, corporate matri-groups in the forests of Ghana and the serial endeavours involved in organizing gold mining, forest clearance, extensive agriculture, and the Asante state.[8] For the Luo of western Kenya, the picture presented by the evidence of such alliances in the sequences of occupation and conquest of *gunda* Gangu is quite at variance with the existing body of literature.

Evans-Pritchard, Southall, Ogot, Whisson, Ochieng', Wilson, and Blount[9] — all of whom did research in Siaya — were followed by a number of secondary sources (including the present writers' earlier work on the Luo past) in stressing the patrilineage as the fundamental organizing unit within Luo society, and segmentation as the essential process of combination and separation. In so presenting patrilineality as a timeless feature, and therefore as a central motor of Luo experience, scholars have consciously or unconsciously suppressed observations of the dynamics of other forms of association and other possibilities of collective activity. By giving prominence to patrilineality, powerful presumptions are introduced into the study of the Luo past concerning the nature of action and the explanation of event.[10] The growth of community, the expansion of population, the formation of Luo 'nation', and the construction of political movements are comprehended in terms of segmentary kinship processes writ large through endless repetition and agglomeration.

Let us return to the *gundni* and look more closely at the process of construction of identity and group over time, and also look at the ways in which familiar social categories, consonant with a Luo ideology of patrilineality and segmentation, are continuously reworked. Some people today recall that the first *gunda bur* was Ligala in Samia, which is considered to be the first settled compound of the Luo in Kenya. The builders and occupants of the original Ligala are remembered as the general Jok group, whose membership included the Alego, Seje, and Nyinek peoples. The new *gundni bur* which they and their descendants dug were all named Ligala and the actual process of starting a new settlement was and is described as *goyo ligala*, which could be translated as 'cutting a new foundation'. The first physical operations in starting a new compound are an important and ceremonial occasion; and though one today does not excavate a trench, as in the *gunda bur*, one still speaks of *goyo ligala*.

As the population of the *gunda* expanded, as a modicum of security was established in the area, and as wealth was reckoned less exclusively in such easily portable goods as cattle, the children of the *gunda* established *dala* or new homesteads (and ones less well fortified) outside the *gunda*. The expanding local community is referred to as *gweng*. This *gweng* was not a residential unit of agnatic kin. Its basis was in the formation of alliances, developing from strategic considerations; alliances organized to seize, and then enlarged to hold the *gunda*.

Early on, the space of the *gweng* was the rising slopes on both sides of the *pap* (low-lying grazing lands) with the *pap* controlled by the *gweng*. As agriculture was extended and gained increasing importance to the survival of the *gweng*, the *pap* became a 'no-man's-land' or common ground, marking a boundary between *gwenge* (plural). The *gundni*, though walled, and the *gwenge*, though bounded, were surely never isolates. The key to their survival in the dangerous world of the seventeenth and eighteenth

centuries was in securing support and labour through incor-
porative strategies and through securing alliances across space
with other settlements.

For example, the utilization of the alliance networks of the
gweng in long-distance contacts was the motor of the Nyanza-
Samia iron trade.[11] These alliances allowed safe travel, the
individual utilizing interlocking social networks or *gwenge*,
through affinal relations and the *luth* travel insignia. Extensively
and routinely utilized long-distance networks — heavily 'traf-
ficked' networks — established the working bases of *ogendini*
('tribes') (sing. *oganda*) such as Jo-Alego and Jo-Ugenya and may,
later on, have been steadily extended in range to bring a feeling
of enlarged oneness and kinship to areas much wider than the
ogendini territories. The rich materials of history, of past contacts, alliances, old marriages, coalitions, and descent, could be
sifted and interpreted to provide an ideological and rhetorical
basis for such constructions as the *gweng* and the *oganda*.

A bridge is constituted between alliance as a social process
and consensual rationalization as an ideological process. This
bridge worked to enhance the reception of migrants in new areas
by emphasizing known, consensual and general identities rather
than localized and particular ones. As marriage alliances were
constructed over greater distances, the integument of relations
between here and there was progressively thickened, and the
geographical dimensions of an individual's known field of relations were considerably widened. The movement from here to
there, establishing oneself in a new place, was considerably
facilitated, encouraging further migrations. Greater unity was
accorded some migrating groups (for example, the Jo-
Karuchuonyo) as they constructed a broad working identity. In
looking further at the past of Luo groups and communities in
western Kenya, we must ask to what extent the large lineal group
was the outcome, rather than the basis, of social activity over
an extended period of time.

The study of migration

Over the past two decades, the migrations of human populations have come to command a predominant place in the research
of a number of historians of pre-colonial Africa. These historians
have seen migration in Africa as the principal means by which
cultural practices and institutions have been transferred across
the continent. Migration has been recognized as the initial and
traceable element in the introduction of new technologies into
new regions of settlement and of the remaking of the physical *15*

terrain of Africa. Migrations have been held to hold the key to the formation of centralized polities — chiefdoms and kingdoms — in different parts of Africa.

Across much of Africa, slave-raiding and tribute-raiding caused large populations to take flight and closed off areas to settlement. Likewise, desiccations, epidemics, and infestations engendered large-scale migrations. Migrations, big and small, transformed the locational geography of Africa, building concentrations of population here, leaving empty corridors there. Changes in land tenancy, service, marriage, household organization, inheritance, livestock keeping, land management, and community governance were consequences of the demographic effects of migration. Migrations challenged the authority of rules and the ideological models of lineage and extended family. And migrations held the potential of constituting active and residual regional and ethnic organizations.[12]

This interest in migration has gone hand-in-hand with a new generation of oral historical work. Historians of Africa standing amidst a 'parched' documentary landscape have been seeking not only new bodies of evidence but also contexts of event through which the work of reconstructing the past may be pursued. In search of new evidence, but also following trends more generally in the field of history, historians of Africa have shifted some of their attention from kings and courts to the population at large, and perspectives have shifted from 'top-down' to 'bottom-up'.

Traditions of, evidence on, migration and settlement have become signal documents locating streams of human population in space and, ostensibly, in time. This genre of study — sometimes called 'migrations and settlements' — has come under occasional waves of criticism as antiquarian adventure or as producing an historical literature so complex as to defy comprehension by even the gifted reader.

Some twenty years have passed since the publication of Bethwell Allan Ogot's *History of the Southern Luo*, which was based on a doctoral dissertation accepted by the University of London in 1965. Ogot's work indicated the value of extending the collection and analysis of oral testimony beyond the courts and capitals of eastern Africa to populations at large and to societies with less visible centralized institutions, or none at all. The broad argument of Ogot's monograph was that histories of such populations or such societies could be written. Ogot gave clarity to tortuous traditions of migration of the myriad Luo-speaking families and clans that he found among the Padhola of eastern Uganda and the Luo of western Kenya.

While Ogot offered a viewable portrait of the horizontal mobility of the groups, lineages, and families that came to make up important elements of the Luo-speaking populations of eastern Uganda and western Kenya, his study is little concerned with the character of the migrating families themselves. Like the larger and less-honed work of J. P. Crazzolara[13], Ogot's *History of the Southern Luo* is essentially nomenclatural. The central technique of the research was genealogical and the central mode of reconstruction was name-linkage.

Both in Ogot's monograph and Crazzolara's earlier publications, cultural forms and institutions are given but fleeting attention. The very character of their treatment is a strong reflection of the character of their primary evidence, the 'historical traditions' of families and clans. These traditions — or perhaps more accurately testimonies containing information on the past — tend to be immediate and parochial in orientation. Culture is not explicated, made overt, but is rather assumed in the transactions between orator and listener. This silent character of the text is transferred to the monograph.

The cultural forms and structural arrangements that lie quietly beneath the surface of the work of Ogot and Crazzolara are of considerable interest to historians of pre-colonial eastern Africa.[14] First, what we do know of the early history of the region suggests that Luo-speaking groups made a significant impact among non-Luo-speaking populations right across northern and eastern Uganda and western Kenya over the past four and a half centuries. To understand the centrality and dominance that migrant Luo often appear to have achieved, or have been accorded by others, one must look beneath the surface of the details on horizontal mobility.

Second, there is an interest in understanding variations in culture among historic Luo-speaking populations and in sorting out indications of distinctions in material life and social organization. One seeks to move beyond the simple construction or presumption that myriad Nilotic Luo-speakers from the southern Sudan to northern Tanzania shared a common culture. The challenge for historians is one of cracking open this language-culture homology through the analytical operation of disaggregation.

Third, there is an interest in identifying the webs of association and exchange that endured in time, spanned considerable distance, and connected populations and resources later distinguished by evolving political and administrative boundaries. Migrations in the African past imply breaks between old and new settlements, between 'core' and descendant populations. The presumption that migrations reveal a social topography of broken relations deserves challenge, or at least further discussion, for western Kenya and for other parts of Africa.

Because for migrant groups the cultural forms and institutions

17

are not embedded in the physical space around them, but rather in deep, unconscious structures and principles, their recovery from a remote past is, in fact, difficult. But even given the nominal character of migration traditions, and the nominal quality of the redactions of testimonies on migrations in the past, these are not thereby closed to modes of inquiry that go beyond questions of horizontal mobility and nomenclature.

If, in our close reconstructions of migrations, we are in fact reconstructing forms of action in the past, then we may at the same time be isolating and capturing particular instances of behaviour. It is therefore possible that the study of migrations within a specific and narrow field might reveal patterns of behaviour, choice, and orientation that are not revealed at an explicit level in narrative tradition. Moreover, such revealed patterns of behaviour may throw stronger light upon the experience of contact among diverse families and provide a better perspective on the three objectives set forward above. The 'Southern Luo'-speakers, Ogot's subjects, are a superb case in point, for they may be studied in an enduring Luo-speaking context in western Kenya (Alego) and in Padhola in eastern Uganda and in a non-Luo-speaking context in nearby Busoga (Bukooli) in eastern Uganda.

Bukooli and Alego

The *gundni bur* just north and north-east of Lake Gangu lie in the midst of an historic migration corridor extending from the sphere of semi-deciduous forest and banana cultivation of southern and south-central Busoga in Uganda through the moist savanna and occasional dry grassland to the higher and moister lands of Kakamega and the lower and drier lands close by the Winam Gulf. Historians have recorded a myriad of testimonies from individuals who note that their ancestors passed through this corridor into what became western Kenya. Important places in the migrational passages of the ancestral groups from the north and north-west are remembered and placed before the historian.

The close study of these memories of migration into western Kenya, and of the settlement patterns and economic orientations implied by the migrational evidence, has been linked to a parallel study of the experience of formerly Luo-speaking groups in Busoga who were themselves migrants from the north. The precise relationships between these groups 'left behind in Busoga' and those groups venturing into western Kenya have been reconstructed. From this comparison, it has been possible to reflect on the 'behaviour' of Luo-speaking groups in a setting where they eventually ceased to speak Luo (Busoga) and the behaviour of the 'same groups' in Luo-speaking western Kenya.[15]

The study reveals a distinction between two broad categories of ancestral Luo-speakers — Owiny, or Owiny Karuoth, and Omolo — in both eastern Busoga (Bukooli specifically) and western Kenya (Alego specifically). The broad categories of 'Owiny' and 'Omolo' have been constructed, or reconstituted, out of the analysis of relationships of kinship among a number of small groups, lineages, and clans, which do not themselves explicitly indicate their own relationships and which, for some, do not use or recognize the 'Owiny' or 'Omolo' terms.

The observations of behaviour in the Bukooli and Alego areas together suggest that the 'Owiny' and 'Omolo' groups came from two distinct worlds, with strikingly different orientations toward cattle, land, settlement, power, and social relations. Owiny groups appear to have expressed a commitment to pastoralism and a valorization of cattle only in rituals of governance. By contrast, Omolo groups, over a considerable period of migration and settlement, were actively involved with cattle and a domestic economy based on livestock, pasturage, and mobility.

From early on in their experiences in Bukooli and Alego, Owiny groups also associated themselves with fixed sites of settlement and maintained a strong attachment to their earliest settlement sites over a long period of time. For Omolo groups such identifications with fixed sites of settlement were long delayed. The Owiny groups, or Owiny individuals, were from an early period surrounded by non-Luo followers and supporters. Such an attraction is not noted at all in respect to the migrational experience of the Omolo groups. The Owiny groups appear to have achieved, or to have been accorded, a hereditary ascription of elevated status from an early time and wherever they went in the general area of Bukooli and Alego. Such an elevation of status is not noted for any Omolo group until quite late in the pre-colonial period. Where polities have developed around the ancestral Owiny, there are no examples of a tradition or story indicating that the Owiny achieved their domination through a situational experience. For each of the few cases in which Omolo groups achieved such domination, there is an explicit account of a situational experience through which they achieved power.

In addition to offering a challenge to the historian's notion of 'Luo-ness', this identification of the quite distinctive complexes of qualities associated with Omolo and Owiny groups in seventeenth-century Bukooli and seventeenth- and eighteenth-century Alego brings into sharper focus the character of the families and lineages that were to emerge as dominant across much of northern, central, and eastern Busoga and in Alego (and therefore has implications for the study of the emergence of these centralized polities). What is disclosed in the observations is that the Owiny groups carried into eastern Bukooli and Alego an aura of prestige and particular ideas of domination and subordination that would play crucial roles in the institutionalization of political control in later generations. The observations suggest that this complex of ideas and prestige was the source rather than the consequence of the elaboration of the retinues and the emergence of new centres of authority.

In Luo discourse, the idea of domination is expressed as *karuoth*, the royal family, or the dominant family, in a community. The stress is upon the exalted status of a potentially broad, collateral group based on kinship rather than upon an individual attribution of authority. The *karuoth* idea gives emphasis to inherent and hereditary capacity, and in so doing surrounds all members of a family with an aura of privilege. That this idea itself had no particular relationship to centralized authority must be underlined, for the interweaving of ideas of distinction and prominence and a principle of inheritance of status meant, in essence, that authority was unable to crystallize at particular nodes. Rather, authority constantly flowed outward to new male members and to new lineage segments and to new settlements, camps and enclosures. We can see the play of the principle of *karuoth* within seventeenth-century Busoga, for everywhere an Owiny group went, its members projected a pre-eminence, if only temporarily.

This argument — that particular ideas concerning domination were carried into the eastern Busoga by Owiny groups and were later carried by Owiny figures and their clients and followers across central and northern Busoga and into Alego — is at some variance with Ogot's discussion of state formation[16] and with his later argument in the *History of the Southern Luo*. The former piece was devised as an attack on the 'Hamitic' explanation of the appearance of East African kingdoms. In arguing this point, Ogot took a 'situationalist' stance, seeing the emergence of states controlled by Luo-speakers, or former Luo-speakers, as a 'result of a small, well-organized group successfully imposing its rule over a disorganized majority.'[17] This key sentence has limited our explanatory power. We learn little of the structural and organizational arrangements connoted in the expression 'well-organized group' nor are we provided any deeper picture of the process of 'successfully imposing . . . rule'. While the experience of one Omolo group in Busoga (the Wakooli group) may appear to fit this model, such is not the whole story — even in outline form — of the Owiny groups in Busoga.

That there may have been deep cultural orientations giving shape, motion, and direction to the 'well-organized group' does not necessarily mean that we have to look back to an ancient and intangible idea of authority handed down among descendant Luo-speaking groups from some remote 'cradleland' of culture and ethnicity. The Owiny groups in seventeenth-century Busoga and in seventeenth- and eighteenth-century Alego simply betray earlier experience of dealing successfully with 'other peoples', specifically agricultural populations. If they are pastoralists when they reach eastern Busoga, the Owiny groups are also ready to exchange, in quick order, an emotional attachment toward cattle and a pastoralist's mobility for fixed sites of settlement, agriculture, dominance, and ritualization of pastoral tradition. The Omolo groups, by contrast, are slow to make adjustments to the new possibilities of settled communities, are reluctant to surrender a seemingly parochial pastoralist existence for fixed sites of settlement, even where, as in Alego, their arrival may have had a momentous impact on the existing community. They betray in their traditions an inexperience in dealing with settled, agricultural peoples.

Given these distinctions, some of the complex migratory traditions of the Luo groups, which refer to movements prior to the eastern Busoga settlements, begin to make sense. The traditions of the Owiny groups, for example, indicate a strong association with areas of north-western Uganda and the northern margins of Bunyoro, where agricultural communities have apparently been present since at least the beginning of the second millennium A.D. Some, though not all, traditions of Omolo groups point to north-eastern Uganda, to the enduring pastoralist sphere between the Agooro mountains in the southern Sudan and Mount Elgon in eastern Uganda.

On the basis of a variety of evidence, generally independent of these findings on eastern Uganda and western Kenya, historians working in the early 1970s on the past of northern Uganda made a sharp distinction between what they have chosen to call 'western Luo' and 'eastern Luo' migrations.[18] This would seem to be a useful locus for the re-examination of not merely the timing and geography of migration of Luo-speakers but, more importantly, of the meaning of 'Luo' culturally and the implications of the 'eastern' and 'western' distinction.

For this present study of Siaya, then, the evidence available suggests that broad and significant distinctions among Luo-speaking peoples appeared in the narrow and critical channel of seventeenth- and eighteenth-century pasturages and settlements just north of Lake Gangu. Questions are thereby raised concerning the ways in which a *volk* emerged out of a diverse and discontinuous population to produce not only a people or nation, the 'JoLuo' — with their routines, rituals, laws, beliefs, and consciousness of identity — but also the concept of a collective descent from the 'JoKanyanam', the people of the rivers and lakes, the people of 'the Luo cradleland in the Nile Valley' of the Sudan.

NOTES

1. Oginga Odinga, *Not Yet Uhuru: An Autobiography* (New York, Hill and Wang, 1969).
2. Peter C. Oloo (Aringo), 'History of settlement: the example of Luo clans of Alego (1500-1918)', BA dissertation, University of East Africa (University College, Nairobi), April 1969, p. 9.
3. A reconstructed sequence of occupants of *gunda* Gangu, developed from a series of interviews by David William Cohen in Alego, for example, runs as follows: 'The Boro people, Kateg people, Alego people of Uyowa, the Kakan people, Ager's people, Lang'o people, Seje people and Nyinek people...'
4. This common theme of a 'descent' from Sudan is heard in most lineage chronicles and is found in the principal published work by authors from western Kenya: Samuel Ayany, Shadrack Malo, William Ochieng', and B. A. Ogot. See Chapter 2 below.
5. B. A. Ogot, *History of the Southern Luo* (Nairobi, East African Publishing House, 1967); also, see David William Cohen, 'The river-lake Nilotes from the fifteenth to the nineteenth century', in B. A. Ogot (ed.), *Zamani: A Survey of East African History* (Nairobi, East African Publishing House and Longman, new edn, 1974), pp. 136-49.
6. Ben G. Blount and Richard T. Curley, 'The southern Luo languages: a glottochronological reconstruction', *Journal of African Languages*, 9 (1970), 1, pp. 1-18; A. N. Tucker and M. A. Bryan, *Linguistic Analyses. The Non-Bantu Languages of North-Eastern Africa* (London, Oxford University Press, 1966); and the detailed linguistic studies of A. J. H. Odhiambo, Duncan Okoth-Okombo, and Lucia Omondi.
7. Principally, E. E. Evans-Pritchard, 'Luo clans and tribes', *Rhodes-Livingstone Journal*, 7 (1949), pp. 24-40; and Aidan Southall, *Lineage Formation Among the Luo* (London, Oxford University Press, 1952). For a most important study of a Luo lineage as a process of mediation of individual and collective interests, see David A. Goldenberg, 'We are all brothers: the suppression of consciousness of socio-economic differentiation in a Kenya Luo lineage', PhD dissertation, Brown University, 1982.
8. Ivor Wilks, 'Land, labour, capital and the forest kingdom of Asante', in J. Friedman and M. J. Rowlands (eds), *The Evolution of Social Systems* (Pittsburgh, University of Pittsburgh Press, 1977), pp. 487-534.
9. In addition to the works cited above, one is thinking here of William Ochieng', *A History of the Kadimo Chiefdom of Yimbo in Western Kenya* (Nairobi, East African Literature Bureau, 1975); Gordon Wilson, *Luo Customary Law and Marriage Customs* (Nairobi, Government Printer, 1968); and Ben G.

Blount, 'Agreeing to agree on genealogy: a Luo sociology of knowledge', in Mary Sanches and Ben G. Blount (eds), *Sociocultural Dimensions of Language Use* (New York, Academic Press, 1975), pp.117-35.

10. David Parkin, *The Cultural Definition of Political Response: Lineal Destiny among the Luo* (London, Academic Press, 1978), appears to lean toward supplanting the expression 'Luo segmentary system' with 'Luo polysegmentary lineage culture'. Parkin set himself the task of understanding how a 'system' worked through the operations of 'culture'. Parkin sees forceful paradigms — expressed in routinized, preferred, and constraining verbal concepts, operating as codes — giving shape both to the ways in which social practices and norms are discussed and the ways in which they actually operate. Parkin notes that '. . . Luo culture [has] operated at least the past hundred years according to a dominant paradigm of family and lineage expansion and segmentation through the accumulation of exchange of women and bridewealth. The paradigm is nowadays expressed more in the attempt to push one's progeny into acquiring jobs and education than land and cattle, but it is still the ultimate referent of thought, speech, and action.' (p. 315) Parkin's is an important and valuable argument for the present discussion in that he points to the complex underpinnings of what has been taken to be 'custom'. And he assists us further in demonstrating how a paradigm of lineality or segmentation gives an integrating form to the knowledge and exposition of diverse action in the Luo past. Parkin leaves us with the challenge of comprehending the tension between action or event or process in the Luo past and the interpretation of the phenomena in Luo discourse.

11. See the valuable study on the pre-colonial iron industry in western Kenya: Priscilla O. Were, 'The origin and growth of the iron industry and trade in Samia (Kenya)', BA dissertation, University College, Nairobi, 1972.

12. David William Cohen, 'Doing social history from *pim*'s doorway', in Olivier Zunz, *Reliving the Past: The Worlds of Social History* (Chapel Hill, University of North Carolina Press, 1985), p. 215.

13. J. P. Crazzolara, *The Lwoo* (Verona, Editrice Nigrizia, 1950, 1951, and 1954).

14. The discussion that follows draws upon David William Cohen, 'Luo camps in seventeenth century eastern Uganda: the use of migration tradition in the reconstruction of culture', *Sprache und Geschichte in Afrika (SUGIA)*, 5 (1983), pp. 145-75, a paper prepared for and presented to the International Congress of Africanists, Addis Ababa, 1973.

15. ibid.

16. B. A. Ogot, 'Kingship and statelessness among the Nilotes', in Jan Vansina, R. Mauny, and L. V. Thomas (eds), *The Historian in Tropical Africa* (London, Oxford University Press, 1964), pp. 284-302.

17. ibid., p. 298.

18. Much of this work was done under the direction of Professor J. B. Webster, then (in the early 1970s) chairman of the Department of History, Makerere University, and was to have been published in the lamentably stalled *History of Uganda*, Vol. 1.

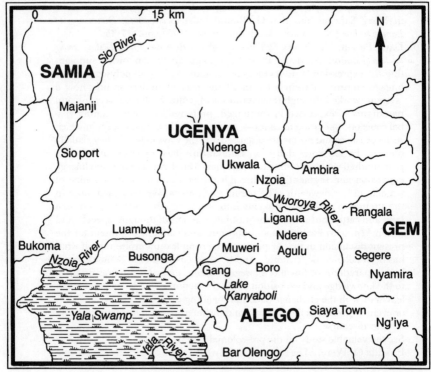

Map 2 Upper Siaya (Alego, Gem, Samia, Ugenya)

The Construction of   II
Boundaries

'Of course . . . Odongo does not feel at home because *home* is where the placenta is.'

People in Siaya say that the weak and awkward are those whose placentas were buried outside their respective homesteads and, worse still, those whose placentas were buried away from the lands of familiar people. They refer to these individuals as *jooko*, the 'outsiders'. Indeed, those who are thought of as weak and clumsy may be referred to as *biero* (placenta), as in the remark 'Nene oyik dhano to owe biero'('we buried the human being and left alive the placenta'). In contrast, those whose placentas are buried within their respective homesteads are seen to belong, to be upright, to be secure.

Biero, then, becomes part of the constitution of boundaries between those born and raised on familiar ground and those unrecognized, or coming from outside the lands of familiar people. Doubt is cast on the claims of those not traceable to the homestead. They are *jooko*.

Importantly, the value of the homestead is articulated in each discussion of *biero*. Tension is introduced into the thinking of young people considering moving elsewhere to seek work or new lands to settle. They are exposed to the likelihood that they will be received as *jooko* elsewhere; and they are pressed to discover and secure the support of known relations in the new setting. Intimate concerns and discussions in the homestead feed into the construction of enduring social and ethnic boundaries, in Siaya and elsewhere.

The discussion of *biero* also places pressure on young women to return to their country homes to give birth. And the *biero* discourse is part of the pressure placed on young men from Siaya to return to the countryside to enhance the *simba* (the 'bachelor's house') and to make investments in the countryside. While composing an ideology reaffirming the country homestead, concepts such as *jooko* and *biero* are joined to other issues and interests. 25

Gestures and salutations

There is a Dholuo saying: 'Ka Lang'o ok kun e kuon.' 'One cannot be coy, or choosy, about a Lang'o goodwill gesture.'

This saying, or proverb, refers to the manners of association with others. If the 'Lang'o', the others, offer you meat you do not hesitate in accepting. If you hesitate, the 'Lang'o' will eat it.

It is understood that the 'Lang'o' does not invite you to 'possess'; rather, he invites you to 'share'. The realms of manners between 'us' and 'them' are exposed as different. The proverb reminds the 'us' that in this setting of tension, in the interaction with the other, one should accept the rhythm, the etiquette, the presentation of the other group. An implication is that to abstain is to lose all opportunity. The still deeper meaning is that 'I', as one of 'us', improve my position, or in difficult times survive, by acknowledging, accepting, the terms of the 'other'. One's identity as 'us' is articulated, reinforced, by accepting the terms, manners, routines, of the 'other'.

There is marvellous and powerful paradox in the meanings and intentionalities of this proverb. It has its hidden history. The proverb exclaimed and instructed about the boundary between 'us' and the 'Lang'o' even as, one hundred to three hundred years ago, the Omolo, and other groups possibly referred to as Lang'o at one time or place, were brought within the fold of Dholuo-speaking communities. In another way, the proverb reiterates the power of everyday life in the constitution of ethnic boundaries and identities.

[A] ... factor which restricts the [Luo] children's mobility is the practice of Luo mothers or mother-surrogates of telling children that they will be taken by a lion or a *jalango* if they stray far from the homestead. The term *jalango*, in this particular area, was a reference term for Masai, who had a common territorial boundary with the Luo. The children are cautioned also to be wary of strangers who visit the homestead when the parents are away, again for the same reason, i.e. that the children may be stolen.[1]

Today, the Siaya man or woman participates and derives his and her identity from a network of affective relations with brother, uncle, grandfather, in-law, friend, if not also from that little homunculus that resides on her own or his own shoulder. The individual's identity is crucial in terms of the structuring of communication, civility, and co-operation. The salutation or greeting of one person by another provides the context for initial conversation. An assembly of elders playing Ajua at Boro will greet a returning member of the urban salariat through all his simultaneous identities. The structure, in regard to a man coming upon this assembly, may run as follows:

How are you?

The son of Gangu? [referring to an ancient settlement — *gunda bur*];

The son of Boro? [the identification of a present locational reference];

The son of Agutu? [bringing notice of a respected mother];

The son of Karuoth? [referencing a clan identity];

The son of the rulers? [referring to the claims to ancient domination and present legitimacy of the lineage or clan of the traveller];

The nephew to the Usonga people? [referencing a prestigious pedigree];

The cousin of Okoth the Night Runner? [referring to the relevance of a shared story of bravado];

The son of the people who roasted crocodile? [a humouring and at the same time respectful glance at a brave reputation];

The son of the brewers of the sausage tree? [a joking reference to stories of revelry];

Our son? [a summary and empowering implication that the traveller is one of us].

Each one of these terms of address contains traces of history, deep or shallow, shared and individual. The returning salary-earner finds his locus by recognizing this repertoire. The village meets him at the bus-stop and resocializes him into his people (*yawa*), his patrimony (*dalawa*), his physical and social past (*thurwa*), and to a sociable and discursive language. In the following two weeks or so, the traveller-come-home will traverse the landscape 'greeting' people, visiting his maternal kin, mourning those who had died since he was last home, and entertaining his friends, in the process perhaps seeking out a bride. This social and physical reproduction of his identity is squeezed into his two weeks of vacation.

This web of salutation simplifies a complex situation, because it commences with the individual at the centre of the greeting, but then it comes to envelop those present, those saluting; in reality, it is society saluting itself, or better, saluting its values and its present social categories through the greeting of new or old friends, in-laws, or kins.

In Siaya the individual is synonymous with the stranger, an alien, possibly even an enemy. It is the stranger who has to answer to the question: 'In ng' a?' ('Who are you?') You do not in an important sense exist until you reveal your networks and, more importantly, until this network can be verified by your interrogators. Does anyone present recognize any of your claims as well-founded? If so, there is validation. Even if it is a group of persons being questioned, there is a validation test that is requisite to the recognition of the existence of this group of persons. 'Whose people are you?' might be answered by the response 'Sijenyi's people'; validation is required; then a recognition of the group. Identity then is the composition of oneself by others in a constellation.

In the twentieth century, there have, certainly, been some reformulations of this 'identity parade'. For one, the state has attempted to pin persons down to a sublocational identity, an 'official identity' inscribed on the Kenyan Identity Card. The Kenyan Identity Card registers individuals in terms of sublocations; as presumptive maximal lineages. For example, the Liganwa/Agulu people are listed as living in Koyeyo sublocation. In situations like that west of Boro, where there is a known, considerable mixing of descent groups, the state has created both a sublocation and an identity for them.

In another way, the state has intervened to take areas of extreme heterogeneity of social identity and create identities, as with the two sublocations Ojwando A and Ojwando B in central Alego. The Ojwando means, literally, 'mixed bag', a fictive and deliberately structured identity for anyone in need of one. The creation of sublocations for Ojwando groups in Alego, Yimbo, and Karachuonyo is itself a testimony to the conscious 'invention of tradition' by the colonial state.[2]

What we also have is a situation where the Alego Karuoth clans have had to retrench their dominance by emphasizing their prior rights to land through the invention of their history. The emphasis on the owner of the land, *won piny*, can be seen to be at odds with our original construct of *gunda bur*. The distillation of one-time usage into permanent occupancy requires a reworking of history. One example will suffice. Within the space of the last one hundred and fifty years or so, the present *gunda* Warinda in Liganua has been occupied, in ascending order, by the Karuoth, Kakeny, Yiro, and Abakolwe clans of western Kenya. But the reworked history tends toward the suppression of the stories of these former occupants, and the heroic aspect of how Warinda and his patrilineage captured the *gunda* emerges as the most prominent telling of its past. Even his allies — members of the Uranga and Kagwa clans, who made possible the taking of the *gunda* — have, in Liganua, shed their specific, distinctive knowledge of their contributions to the events in favour of the Warinda episode.

In the case of the Ojwando 'clans', William Ochieng', in his *History of the Kadimo Chiefdom in Yimbo in Western Kenya*,[3] has demonstrated how the Luo-Kadimo clan was invented as the ruling clan by the British at the beginning of this century. This invention, in turn, has inspired the simultaneous invention of competing Kadimo and Ojwando versions of history in Yimbo, which quest has in turn involved the partition of the location and an ongoing competition, at the level of education and *harambee* schools building, between the Dimo and the Ojwando clans.

The Kadimo people . . . aimed at excluding the Ojwando clans from all administrative posts in the location. By manning the administration they benefited from exemption from recruitment as porters, carriers, and very few of them were recruited to go out to work in European plantations, and those of them who could not afford taxes went scot-free, unlike their counterparts, the Ojwando people, who were usually caned, imprisoned or forced to work on the roads . . . the Kadimo people also derived a lot of pride and pleasure from being 'rulers over barbarians'.[4]

Among the issues that arise here is the subtle enmeshing of ideology, identity, and material concerns. In Yimbo, kinship values are not decaying in the contexts of changing communities. Rather, kinship values are being reworked and reinforced in ways in which identity takes the form of economic 'nationalism' within the sublocation, where inequalities — differential access to opportunities — are attributed to social categories, identities which have been substantially invented.

But identity may also develop fortuitously: one patriarch may have, and have educated, ten sons, who in turn will have and possibly educate their forty to fifty sons and daughters. Given the patterns of accumulation associated with education, and also the fact that the educated elites have often married among themselves, a very rapid rate of 'clan' formation is produced. Observers of western Kenya recognize that the late Canon Jeremiah Awori has produced a 'clan' that spans from Samia, is linked via marriage to families in Nyakach, Yimbo, and Bunyore, Busoga, Buganda, Liberia, Malawi, and Britain, and that includes lawyers, financiers, real estate developers, and journalists, with occasional dabblers in politics both in Kenya and Uganda. This pattern has been replicated many times in Siaya.

The Luo refer to this process as *nya* (spreading out). Education is not the only opportunity structure implicated in the appearance and growth of new 'clans'. Traders and wholesalers have met at the market place and created enduring linkages. What one sees in these processes is the convergence of ideology and identity, but not only through patrilineal relationships, and not necessarily towards the wider 'tribal' or 'ethnic' reference categories.

Another issue that arises has to do with the *uses of history*. The invention of sublocations has involved the invention of sublocational history. The legal processes of land adjudication and titling in Siaya have involved the re-enactment of family and lineage histories of the nineteenth century, and perhaps from even earlier. The take-off point is itself contentious. Where the models of Luo society in the work of historians and anthropologists have been firmly patrilineal, in land litigation one's identity is probed

29

both patrilineally and matrilineally. In the process, history explodes silences. The one who was an uncle today is reproduced as an outsider, *ng'ato nono*, tomorrow, with no patrimony, because in reality his ancestors were subordinates (*misumba*) of a founding, self-legitimating lineage; or his ancestor was actually sired by an itinerant Sakwa or Maragoli medicine man, like the Nyamwanda cluster in Sakwa; or he was actually conceived premaritally, so he is the 'child of *simba*', with no claims to the patrimony, like the Kagilo cluster in Gem. Here is historical discourse in everyday life disaggregating, unscrambling strands and segments, valorizing this one, devaluing that one.

Western-trained historians may object to our usage of the word 'history' to refer to these situationally invoked memories. Yet the more generally used, and consensually understood term, *tradition* — particularly as defined by historians such as Jan Vansina[5] and David Henige[6] — does not sit easily with our sense — and with the student of Luo sociolinguistics, Ben Blount's, presentation — of historical accounts in western Kenya as intensely negotiated and arbitrated. For Blount,[7] the knowledge of individuals — read 'elders' — is arbitrated. The arbitration is intense because the past is brought to bear upon the untangling and resolution of a variety of critical conflicts. The arbitration sessions in which elders frequently find themselves as actors are moments of 'workshop history'; and this is so whether the sessions are concerned with establishing lineage seniority, the priority of various non-kin relations, land usufruct, or genealogy generally. The yields of these workshops in turn depend on the models of society at hand. Without oversimplifying, this consensual model — the statist, harmonious, and enclosed model of the clan — is but one of the several available models.

The Luo still think very much in terms of their history. When a dispute is being discussed, the whole historical context is brought out, and the relationships between the individuals examined. The object is to remove the source of tension, rather than to give a juridical answer to a legal problem.[8]

In such sessions, history is addressed, received, and presented as a material of power. There is an economy of history production, as well as a sociology of history production, and at every point identity, the constitution of a group, who one really is, are questions constantly addressed. What is clear is that there is real dis-coordination and contention in the holdings of knowledge on the Siaya past.

If the production of history in Siaya constitutes an important force, it is also being reconstituted as texts through specific processes of stylization. The genealogy or lineage chronicle produced in Blount's laboratory resembles closely the text of the guild historian's field interview in Siaya. The received and recorded text is cleansed of the debates and nuances that produce Blount's genealogy. The rich commotion of the past, and the equally rich and commotional knowledge of history, escapes the oral narration as nomenclature and the simplified genealogical map give structure to the oral text. Diverse and incongruent elements are condensed into, or suspended from the text, and, perhaps in important ways, this text composition, with its exposed structure, comes to be naturalized as the archaic, classic, remnant, and, indeed, only form of historical exposition.

This is not to mean that large, important reservoirs of knowledge of past 'disappear into oral texts'; indeed there is no reason to assume that memory is depleted as individuals recite or compose texts. But a characteristic form of exposition is affirmed, reified. A method or methodology is implicated. And it is a method full of closures and silences. The process of articulation of historical knowledge as lineage chronicle is reminiscent of the process of producing a photographic record of a collective activity in Siaya in which the subjects quickly recompose position, posture, and gesture into a formal group portrait... remaking the effort of the photographer to record a 'natural scene' into a conventional and, by routine, a naturalized portrait of kin and neighbours.

Piny and nation

At another level, beyond the enclosure, neighbourhood, sublocation, or clan, is the *piny*, the territory. The works of E. E. Evans-Pritchard and Aidan Southall imply that such territorial units were fairly distinct by the end of the nineteenth century. Indeed, in 1949, Evans-Pritchard wrote that 'Each Luo tribe (*piny*), coterminous in the main . . . with the present administrative location, was an autonomous unit.'[9] There were, in this view — which many Luo today share — Alego, Gem, Asembo, and Sakwa as examples of territories or domains; and there were, in this same view, individuals and groups identifying themselves or identified as Jo-Alego or Jo-Ugenya. The presentation of pre-colonial western Kenya as a collection of distinct peoples or territories produces a neat organizational structure and conforms to ethnological and ethnographic presentations of peoples elsewhere in Africa. It also fits an implicit logic of *rehearsal*, that these small ethnic units were eighteenth- and nineteenth-century rehearsals for the broadly inclusive ethnic unit of the Luo recognized in the colonial and post-colonial periods.

31

It is the very neatness of Evans-Pritchard's model that generates an uneasiness about its verisimilitude. Contrary evidence is indirect, but powerful. Work by Oloo Aringo[10] on Alego suggests that there were at least three major rivals for control of the general landscape of Alego at the beginning of the twentieth century: the Karuoth, the Kaluo, and the Kakan 'clans'. William Ochieng's material on Yimbo[11] suggests that the very nomenclature of Yimbo-Kadimo (Dimo's Yimbo) was contested by the Ojwando clans, who argued that they were not Dimo's people. The pronounced rivalry within Sakwa, between the Nyasmwa and Nyibinya groups, likewise suggests a contested terrain. Northern Gem in the nineteenth century was really a war-zone between Luo-speaking and non-Luo-speaking groups, while the boundaries of Ugenya contracted toward the southern bank of the River Nzoia through the last century. Michael Whisson and John Lonsdale have shown how the Asembo polity has been such a treacherous terrain that magic alone has held together the people around their chiefdom[12]

This brief collection of evidence from the past forces a review of the original construct. The *piny* were not simple or easy givens, were not of consistent shape or structure, and were perhaps experiencing processes of formation and deformation simultaneously. A question is raised: how did a Gem or an Asembo identity come to be? Blount's sociolinguistic reconstitution of a collective production of a genealogy — by a small group of elders — suggests part of an answer. The collective reconstruction — for example, the agreement that 'this land was originally Alego's' — can be assumed to be adopted by all those present in the historical discussion, though perhaps assertedly so only by those present whose security was not felt to be threatened by the agreement. To yield to the prevailing position in the negotiation is not necessarily a surrender to a point of view, for alternative versions can be carried back out of the discussion, or the negotiation, on the constitution, the authentication of Alego as a *piny*.

Importantly, the Alego or Asembo identity was reinforced by the zoning of people into locations by colonialism. Some saw it as being in their interest to project this formalism back into the past; some saw it in their interest to 'agree to agree' to this expression of the past. Moreover, the chief's *baraza* forged a new identity for people, as weekly the elders walked the main paths to Amoth Owira's *baraza* at Boro. The funeral associations in Nairobi, Mombasa, or Kampala served to reinforce these identities. As the *piny* were worked for their utility in the colonial and post-colonial period, so they were usable models for the simplification of pre-colonial spatial and social organization. The present remade the past, as reworked history legitimated the present.

One must also mention the influence of the outsiders: to the peoples of the highlands and Mombasa areas the migrants from western Kenya were in need of a name — 'WaKavirondo', 'WaPagaya', 'WaRuguru', 'Jaluo' — and all these were tried. It is interesting to note that the first sixteen Luo words recorded in Western literature, in Charles New's *Life, Wanderings and Labours in Eastern Africa* (1873)[13] were provided for him by the Isiria Maasai, who appear to have been then expressing the idea that Ugaya and Luo were separate, distinct entities. In Charles W. Hobley's book,[14] published in 1929, the WaGaya still appeared as a separate language group from the 'Nilotic Kavirondo'. At any rate, between 1873 and the early 1920s, a name tag for these peoples around the Kavirondo (now Winam) Gulf was being forged by the Maasai in contact with travellers, traders, and agents. Here we have a period of about a half century when this population we now refer to as the Luo of Kenya was known by the outsiders, but not through its own address system. One thought is that the early Dholuo-speaking proto-elites began to identify themselves to outsiders as 'Jo-Luo' partly as an expression or signal of rejection of the other names.

The great characteristic of the Wa-Kavirondo as a whole is their honesty; making war upon a neighbouring tribe to take their cattle is considered legitimate, but petty thieving is extremely rare, thus comparing very favourably with the inhabitants of Uganda and Usoga.[15]

But there is more to identity than names, and the political arena appears to be a critical motor in the production of identity. Here the work of David Parkin on the Luo in Nairobi[16] is extremely valuable. Parkin reconstructs the sometime struggles between two political wings of the Luo people in the 1950s and 1960s, which he associates with Tom Mboya and Oginga Odinga respectively. Ideas of *piny* — a 'people', a 'country' — were articulated and elaborated amidst these tensions. Factionalism and struggles within produced a context that generated concepts of broader community and identity, while particular claims of ideological priority pressed home to Luo, and to others, the notion of a global motherland. The early threads of an internally realized and broader Luo identity are likely traceable to the tensions within networks of political and social organizations like the Piny Owacho and the Kavirondo Taxpayers' Welfare Association of the 1920s, the Kisumu Native Chamber of Commerce, the Luo Unions of the 1930s, and the Luo Thrift and

33

Trading Corporation of the 1940s and 1950s.[17]

That this division into two factions [Mboya and Odinga 'constituencies'] with contrasting philosophies meant a great deal to ordinary Luo is instanced by the anger and violence exchanged between their respective supporters during and after the well-attended general meetings held by the Luo Union at Kaloleni Hall at the time. It is also interesting to note the consistency with which Luo report how in many cases the factions actually had a divisive effect on affinal and even sibling relations . . . the Odinga—Mboya contrast represented a summation of alternative ideological possibilities. Odinga ostensibly stood for the collective defence of the Luo community through both 'corporate' radical thought and Luo conservatism. Mboya represented a Western-style meritocracy through the transcension of ethnic conservatism and through individual achievement.[18]

One could stand back from this plethora of complexity at several levels and in multiple contexts and suggest that while the British were busy creating 'tribes' the leading proto-elites were creating the Luo nation. The recurrent reaffirmation of the 'Luo way of life' and the Luo homeland in the proto-elites' discussions eventually defined the core values of this new society. Paul Mboya's text, *Luo Kitgi gi Timbegi*,[19] is a canonization of the asserted culture and behaviour of this new nation. This text became part of the regimen for cultural education in the primary and intermediate schools throughout the 1950s. In the 1960s Oginga Odinga reiterated these core values in the first chapter of his book *Not Yet Uhuru*.[20]

No marriage could be solemnized without the presence of the mother as well as the father . . . We were taught that a good statesman would not give precipitate judgement . . . Elders were men of substance and integrity . . . when they came from leading lineages they did not inherit leadership but had to demonstrate it . . . Diligence yielded prosperity and brought respect, but riches alone did not count for leadership . . . the authority of the elders was much respected, indeed it was never challenged . . . the Luo regarded the land as their mother and the tribe as a whole was the proprietor of all the land in its area . . . Common ownership of the land was accompanied by a system of communal cultivation.[21]

One needs to add that all these tendencies evolved amidst Western missionary enterprise that situated itself in opposition to many cultural practices of the communities. In an important sense, these discourses over moral and modern practice selected and then reified as distinctive elements certain observed practices, for example in the compartmentalizing analysis of marriage arrangements. In turn, these discourses over cultural practice pressured the new elites to be more precise about what were being defined as core values or understandings, which we might term here, temporally, as 'centrepieces'. By the 1940s, these centrepieces were widely shared in Luo-speaking communities broadly across Kenya.

Similarly, perhaps simultaneously, there emerged the concept of the typical man — *JaLuo Asili* — who was identified by his adherence to the 'customs of the land' (*timbe jopiny*) as opposed to the 'customs of the outsiders'. In a crucial sense, the colonial period was a six-decade long colloquy among all sorts of people about culture, markers, boundaries, core values, ethnicities. These core values resonated through the football clubs, the clan associations, and the Luo Union branches. During the 1950s and 1960s, John Cosmas Owade Bala Korguok, broadcasting on the Luo programmes of the state radio, did more than any other person to reiterate these core values. An undoubtedly important institution was the Remington Cup, an inter-district annual football competition that pitted the Luo of Central Nyanza against the Bantu Kavirondo (of North Nyanza) as no other ethnic vehicle could.

The outcome, a sense of a Luo nation within a nation, was not simply, or directly, the product of the rehearsals of previous stages of identity formation. As Parkin has suggested, and as we are arguing, this broad identity was sculpted by real people, in real time, articulating particular and secular interests as well as global ones.

What happens when we set these several points about fluidity in the production, suppression, organization, and utilization of Luo historical knowledge against the understanding of Luo 'oral tradition' received from the guild's professional historians? The terrain of discussion becomes complicated, difficult.

The production of history

Published some twenty years ago, Bethwell Allan Ogot's *History of the Southern Luo*[22] was, and is, an impressive effort to write a history of what one may refer to as the 'whole Luo people of eastern Uganda and western Kenya'. With two decades behind us, we can look back and place the Ogot volume among other works of Luo prose historiography, to try and catch its originality and its nuances, and the ways in which time has remade the book, from a published dissertation to a handbook on the Luo past heavily used by Luo in settling marriage and land disputes. We can also now position other, and earlier, historians of the Luo alongside Ogot, and we can attempt to see how the principal works of early Dholuo and English prose historiography on western Kenya sit among the broader production of history of the people of the region outside the guild of literary producers of history.

We have already noted how the production of history in western Kenya is often and substantially about the constitution   *35* of identity, not just about a 'Luo people' or a 'Luo nation' but also about the constitution of other collective and individual identities in western Kenya, of which the 'Luo nation' is but one. An inquiry into Luo identity is an inquiry into the multiplicity of forms of identity formation in innumerable contexts and at countless moments, from the 'us and them' of settlements in the ancient fortified enclosures of the *gunda bur* just north of Lake Gangu to the 'us and them' in recent debates among Kenyan historians over their place in Mau Mau historiography.

John Lonsdale has termed the constitution of ethnic identity the 'unfinished process of coming to be';[23] to unravel this unfinished process is, as we have discussed, clearly a complex if not impossible project. There is an incompleteness not only of its conclusion, but in the many twists and turns of intermediate and prior integument. There are different intentionalities to unravel and multiple and variably nuanced identities to be caught, decoded, understood. But there are elements that the historian can access, thereby planting his feet firmly upon the broad and important field of history production, for there is no nuancing or expression of identity in western Kenya that does not represent the past or reference a knowledge of the past, and in so doing produce history.

Shadrack Malo is reckoned a founding father of Luo prose historiography. Malo wrote his *Dhoudi Mag Central Nyanza* (first published in 1953)[24] from the chiefs' *barazas* in western Kenya. For Malo, the locational council was the first rendezvous with modern historiography. Malo drew upon the expertise of individuals around the chiefs' *barazas*. Malo's was a history of the Luo people generally, but it was written from, and based upon, the knowledge, stories, testimony, of important men in the precincts and chambers of colonial administration. In this sense, we might term Malo's work not so much a 'tribal history' as a '*tribunal*' one, with the emphasis being upon the power of the tribunes to define their interests within Malo's research. Malo's informants were the location elders, and they in turn hammered out aggregate, consensual histories of the 'major clans' convenient for the time, and for themselves as the local notables. Malo's work raises many issues; among them is the denotation of prime and ancient patrilineages — the Ugenya Kager, the Gem Kojuodhi, and the Alego Seje — running back to Podho and Aruwa in what is now northern Uganda. A chronology of nearly a thousand years is implicated in Malo's presentation of these patrilineages. It is an instance where the twelfth and thirteenth centuries are clearer than the nineteenth century.

When the Luo first arrived in their present homeland, a great number of them passed through Alego. Up to this day there are the fortresses of these sojourners. The early walls of these forts are still clearly visible.

Ramogi, the younger grandson to Ramogi the elder, first arrived at Ramogi Hill (in Yimbo) with his son Jok. He came via Ligala, where the Banyala now live. From there he came to Ramogi Hill, where Jok begat Imbo.

Imbo had nine sons: Mumbo, Nyinek, Rado, Nyikal, Dimo, Nyiywen, Iro, Magak, and Julu. Imbo's descendants are scattered as follows: Mumbo's descendants are in South Nyanza, Dimo's in Central Nyanza, Iro in North Nyanza, Nyikal in Seme location in Central Nyanza, and Julu in Kajulu location in Central.

Mumbo begat Muljuok and Uyawa. Muljuok begat Alego, Chwanya, and Omwa. The descendants of Chwanya and Omwa are the Karachuonyo and the Kanyamwa groups in South Nyanza. Alego begat Seje.[25]

This distinction between the clarity of the remote and the obscurity of the near is observable in work on the Nilotic Luo or 'River-Lake Nilotes' more broadly, for example in the work of Onyango Ku Odongo and J. B. Webster in their *Central Lwo during the Aconya*.[26] Within the guild of professional scholars, and perhaps also outside it, certain agreements have evolved almost unconsciously concerning the principal elements and outlines of Luo history at a chronological distance. For periods nearer to the present, on the other hand, no similar agreements have evolved or are available.

Related to this is the canonization or formalization of a stylized and particularly framed Luo history — presently, importantly, as *the* Luo history, or the only 'knowing' of the accessible Luo past. The history of the 'tribune' was read as the history of the 'tribe' by Malo's audience.

Another historian of the Luo, Samuel Ayany, in his *Kar Chakruok Mar Luo*,[27] first published in 1948, took a different path from that of Malo. Ayany sought a more 'popular' mode, in which potentially every Luo kinship collectivity would represent itself, or be represented, in the 'complete Luo history'. While writing at the same time as Malo, Ayany was looking beyond Malo's centring of the tribunes in his research and presentation. For Ayany, the 'tribe' was produced and confirmed by the totality of segmentary kinship relations. History, for Ayany, lay in aggregating the myriad histories of distinct lineages. For Ayany, the problem was not a model of historical process in the Luo past — for him this was self-evident — the problem was in the limitations of memory and the constraints on research effort that precluded reaching and reconstructing all segments of the 'tribe'.

In this respect, the type of treatment of the past represented by Ayany's work is generally viewed by a wide readership — but not so viewed here — as constrained by the social and cultural limitations on memory and orality rather than by a very selective and specific approach to rendering the past. Early ethnological notions of what a people were and what a history should look like came into specific western Kenya literature through work such as that of Crazzolara and Evans-Pritchard on Nilotic peoples of northern Uganda and southern Sudan. Through them, the 'tribunal process' of history production in western Kenya was remade into a 'tribal process' — the vision of the 'tribe' inscribed in the long, segmentary genealogies of lineage histories. In this sense, in this expounded process of forming new groups, yet remaining as one, the ancient Luo were seen to be rehearsing a modern Luo nationalism, larger and more binding than any political, social, and economic divisions that might appear among them.

This recomposition of what a history should look like drew readers and historians into two critical traps: first, that history could only be the 'history of the tribe'; and, second, that this history was 'this tribe's past'.

Ayany belongs to the second generation of the Luo elites who have, since the 1920s, been continually inventing both a nation (in the *volk* sense of it) and giving this invented nation an invented 'history'. Ayany's work lies midway between that of Malo, a local administrator, and that of Ogot, the first Luo historian of the professional guild. Ogot inherited both the 'tribunal' version of Malo, and Ayany's popular version, in which everyone had a historical place according to his or her position in a genealogy. To these two approaches — the second, in its incontrovertible segmentary logic, had the capacity to envelop the first — Ogot added a Whig interpretation. This held that the Luo have always been marching toward 'Canaan'. He also added a methodology, centring on the carefully constructed and recorded oral interview, which gave the mission of Luo historiography a doorway into academic discourse.

Ogot's *History of the Southern Luo* is in a certain sense Janus-faced. It looks toward the academic shelves, where it has easily found 'a place to feel at home', for it has reintroduced the Luo person into the mainstream of the history of the world. But it also looks toward, without quite tackling, the *gunda bur*, the barely understood, ancient fortified settlement of north-western Siaya and the Uganda—Kenya borderland. The *gunda bur* was the contextual ground of early settlements of the ancestral Luo in western Kenya and the treatment of the *gunda bur* has become the critical core of the entire logic of Luo historiography.

Ogot's work not only offered a reworked perspective on the historical processes of segmentation of a 'homeland' people, but also an opening to the study of the turbulences and contests of the past of western Kenya and eastern Uganda. If Malo and Ayany saw the past as a rehearsal for Luo nationalism in the twentieth century, Ogot's work reads as a rehearsal for deeper inquiry into the seams, crevices, and divides of the Luo past, often involving ancient and lingering disputes from which the historian of the guild, Professor Ogot, could not distance himself.

Malo and Ayany consciously and unconsciously suppressed the signs and substance of dis-coordination and contention in the holdings of the people of Siaya on their past. Their objective was the projection of harmony, their presentation of the Luo past as rehearsals for cultural and political revival and nationalism. Malo and Ayany perhaps had no vision of another kind of history. Ogot disclosed tensions in the past but exposed readers to only a narrow band of the contentious material on the past held by the people of Siaya themselves. Ogot's book does Malo and Ayany one better, for it offers the careful and patient reader a view of a people, a nation, 'Canaan', constructed out of critical tensions and conflicts over land, political domination, and domestic insecurity. That the Ogot volume has been used as a tome on local rights rather than national tradition is a reflection of the power of people in everyday Siaya to produce history and to make history work for them.

Indeed, Ogot's work has stopped one gate short of the *dala*, the contemporary Luo homestead, at the magistrate's courts. Among literate Luo, Ogot's *History* appeals most readily to the lawyers and advocates, as they unravel the migrations, settlements, and wars of the various named lineages and clans. This unravelling occurs within the courtroom, for the purposes of establishing the claims of their clients. That this work of historical scholarship has no other equally ready application in the lives of ordinary people speaks volumes about the processes of knowledge in Siaya. Ogot is not alone in experiencing this unintended diversion of a historical text. Jomo Kenyatta wrote *Facing Mount Kenya*[28] as a charter for Gikuyu nationhood. But its most ready function in Gikuyu society has been in the courts: as an authority on family law, particularly relating to dowry and divorce.

Kenyatta and Ogot may indeed have felt that the primary chapters of their work were not being read closely, or at all, and certainly not as they intended them to be read. But, at minimum, their works are cited as authorities for a specific identity, namely Gikuyu or Luo. They participated in the invention of these ethnic communities — if they were not actually responsible as their foremost inventors. In turn, the communities invented are reworking the texts that contributed to their creation. And this

39

is happening not in terms of the arena of the nation but, most actively and densely, in the arena in which clan identities, lands, status, and individual identity are constantly referenced.

The ways in which Kenyatta and Ogot have been remade into usable works in everyday life brings us back to our initial Luo declaration, with its implicit call for attention to the discourses and manners of everyday life, and it reminds us that the 'unfinished process of coming to be' is not the only purpose of the constant referencing of past.

The tensions between a 'progress' of invented history and a knowledge of past are extraordinarily difficult to map. But we begin to see how individual Luo, within their everyday lives, have referenced their past and affirmed their knowledge of past in constituting who they are. They invoke history in a constellation of personal and collective 'addresses', identities. Even as the people of Siaya attempt to assert their interests,[29] they extend the meanings, the content, of collective identity, working upon a very contemporary name 'JoLuo' and at the same time producing out of a sense of past an ancient collective identity, 'JoKanyanam', people of the rivers and lakes.

NOTES

1. Benny Garell Blount, 'Acquisition of language by Luo children', PhD dissertation, University of California, Berkeley, 1969, p. 27. The historical borderland of Dholuo speech in western Kenya defies detailed mapping due to extensive intermarriage and clientelage among individuals born to different natal speech communities. The historical borderland is also marked by considerable bilingualism. That there were marriage, client, and exchange relations among groups of predominantly different speech does not lessen — in fact may enlarge — the scope for fierce stereotyping of others. For a fine discussion of this point see, Margaret Jean Hay, 'Local trade and ethnicity in western Kenya', *African Economic History Review*, 2, 1 (1975), pp. 7-12.

2. See Eric J. Hobsbawm and Terence Ranger (eds), *The Invention of Tradition*, (Cambridge, Cambridge University Press, 1983) and also John Lonsdale, 'When did the Gusii (or any other group) become a "tribe"?', *Kenya Historical Review* 5 (1975), pp. 123-30. Bogumil Jewsiewicki and Henri Moniot are editing a special number of *Cahiers d'Etudes Africaines* concerned with the use of historical knowledge in the production of ethnic identity in Africa.

3. William Ochieng', *History of the Kadimo Chiefdom in Yimbo in Western Kenya* (Nairobi, East African Literature Bureau, 1975).

4. Ibid., p. 64. For another example of local centralization and differentiation in western Kenya, see the brief treatment of Gem in the nineteenth century in Ralph Herring, D. W. Cohen, and B. A. Ogot, 'The construction of dominance: the strategies of selected Luo groups in Uganda and Kenya', in Ahmed I. Salim (ed.), *State Formation in Eastern Africa* (Nairobi, Heinemann, 1984), pp. 150-2.

5. 'We are . . . ready to define oral traditions as verbal messages which are reported statements from the past beyond the present generation. The definition specifies that the message must be oral statements spoken, sung, or called out on musical instruments only. This distinguishes such sources not only from written messages, but also from all other sources except oral history. The definition also makes clear that all oral sources are not oral traditions. There must be transmission by word of mouth over at least a generation.' Jan Vansina, *Oral Tradition as History* (Madison, University of Wisconsin Press, & London, James Currey 1985), pp. 27-8. As restrictive as this definition may seem — in particular, distinguishing 'tradition' from other verbal forms of history expression — Vansina's earlier definition of *tradition* is more so; compare, *Oral Tradition* (London, Routledge & Kegan Paul, 1965), pp. 19-20.

6. 'Strictly speaking, oral traditions are those recollections of the past that are commonly or universally known in a given culture. Versions that are not widely known should rightfully be considered as "testimony" and if they relate to recent events they belong to the realm of oral history'. David Henige, *Oral Historiography* (New York, Longman, 1982). p. 2.

7. Ben G. Blount, 'Agreeing to agree on genealogy. A Luo sociology of knowledge', in Mary Sanches and Ben G. Blount (eds), *Sociocultural Dimensions of Language Use* (New York, Academic Press, 1975), pp. 117-35.

8. Michael Whisson, *Change and Challenge: A Study of the Social and Economic Changes among the Kenya Luo* (Nairobi, Christian Council of Kenya, 1964), p. 1.

9. E. E. Evans-Pritchard, 'Luo tribes and clans', in E. E. Evans-Pritchard, *The Position of Women in Primitive Societies and Other Essays in Social Anthropology* (New York, The Free Press, 1965), p. 210 (originally published in *Rhodes-Livingstone Journal*, 8 (1949), pp. 24-40). See also Aidan Southall, *Lineage Formation among the Luo* (London, Oxford University Press, 1952).

10. Peter C. Oloo (Aringo), 'History of settlement: the example of Luo clans of Alego (1500-1918)', BA dissertation, University of East Africa (University College, Nairobi), April 1969.

11. Ochieng', *History of the Kadimo Chiefdom*; idem, 'Clan settlement and clan conflict in the Yimbo location of Nyanza, 1500-1915', in B. G. McIntosh (ed.), *Ngano: Nairobi Historical Studies, I* (Nairobi, East African Publishing House, 1969), pp. 48-71; and idem, 'The transformation of a Bantu settlement into a Luo Ruothdom: a case study of the evolution of the Yimbo community in Nyanza up to AD 1900', in Bethwell Allan Ogot (ed.), *Hadith 6: History and Social Change in East Africa* (Nairobi, East African Literature Bureau, 1976), pp. 44-64.

12. M. G. Whisson and J. M. Lonsdale, 'The case of Jason Gor and fourteen others: a Luo succession dispute in historical perspective', *Africa*, 45, 1 (1976), pp. 50-66.

13. Charles New, *Life, Wanderings and Labours in Eastern Africa* (London, Hodder, 1873).

14. Charles W. Hobley, *Kenya: From Chartered Company to Crown Colony* (London, Witherby, 1929).

15. Charles W. Hobley, 'Kavirondo', *The Geographical Journal*, 12 (1896), p. 370.

16. David Parkin, *The Cultural Definition of Political Response: Lineal Destiny Among the Luo* (London, Academic Press, 1978), particularly pp. 214-35. A parallel study of a Luo lineage in a rural setting is David A. Goldenberg, 'We are all brothers: the suppression of consciousness of socio-economic

41

differentiation in a Kenya Luo lineage', PhD dissertation, Brown University, 1982. Goldenberg sees the localized lineage as an interest group or a composite of variable interests of its members (and of their varied articulation with the broader society and economy) as the setting in which Luo ethnicity is in constant process of definition.

17. See Oginga Odinga, *Not Yet Uhuru: An Autobiography* (New York, Hill & Wang, 1967), pp. 61-8; E. S. Atieno Odhiambo, '''Seek ye first the economic kingdom'', a history of the Luo Thrift and Trading Corporation (LUTATCO), 1945-56', in Bethwell Allan Ogot (ed.), *Hadith 5: Economic and Social History of East Africa* (Nairobi, East African Literature Bureau, 1975), pp. 218-56; *idem*, 'Economic mobilization and political leadership: Oginga Odinga and the Luo Thrift and Trading Corporation to 1956', in Aloo Ojuka and William Ochieng' (eds), *Politics and Leadership in Africa* (Nairobi, East African Literature Bureau, 1975), pp. 139-78; and K. M. Okaro-Kojwang', 'Origins and establishment of the Kavirondo Taxpayers' Welfare Association', in B. G. McIntosh (ed.), *Ngano: Nairobi Historical Studies, I*, (Nairobi, East African Publishing House, 1969), pp. 111-28.

18. Parkin, *Cultural Definition* p. 221.

19. Paul Mboya, *Luo Kitgi gi Timbegi* (Nairobi, Equatorial Publishers, 1938).

20. Odinga, *Not Yet Uhuru*, pp. 1-16.

21. Ibid., pp. 11-14.

22. B. A. Ogot, *History of the Southern Luo* (Nairobi, East African Publishing House, 1967).

23. Lonsdale. 'When did the Gusii . . . become a "tribe"', pp. 123-33.

24. Shadrack Malo, *Dhoudi Mag Central Nyanza* (Nairobi, Eagle Press, 1953).

25. Shadrack Malo, *Dhoudi Moko Mag Luo* (Kisumu, Oluoch Publishing House, 1981: a reprint of ibid.), p. 27.

26. Onyango Ku Odongo and J. B. Webster, *The Central Lwo during the Aconya* (Nairobi, East African Literature Bureau, 1976).

27. Samuel Ayany, *Kar Chakruok Mar Luo* (Kisumu, Equatorial Publishers, 1952).

28. Jomo Kenyatta, *Facing Mount Kenya* (London, Secker and Warburg, 1953).

29. Parkin, *Cultural Definition*, pp. 292-94, discusses what he calls the 'stifled cultural debate', the tension between a possibility that 'the long conversation between generations' may break out into an open debate about change and continuity in Luo social life (concerning, for example, monogamy, bridewealth, and education) and the pressure not to permit Luo practice to open itself to wide discussion and criticism. Parkin suggests that it is the persistent use of convenient verbal concepts in Luo speech that 'impose cultural order on disorder', their use constricting broad and open debate. One sees the use of segmentary models in complex discourses as a significant example of what Parkin has postulated. Parkin also recognizes the significance of the position of the urban worker and the urban poor who may see in such debate the unravelling of critical support for self and countryside family. Whether an observer sees Luo discourse over social practice as 'stifled' or 'robust' may reflect the position of the observer.

The Several Landscapes of Siaya

There is something malignant about shanty huts. They go up in the smoke at dawn, spring to life again by twilight. One just cannot keep them down. The Council knows this. Char them as many times as you like and they mushroom back just as many times. Sticks, wire, paper and iron sheets is all it takes. The shanty house is reborn, maybe a bit frail, but quite potent ... People have got to eat, defecate, live.[1]

Kaloleni

Kaloleni is an urban quarter of Nairobi, a 'homeland' of Luo in central Kenya. The community of Kaloleni is not wholly defined by the city fathers of Nairobi as a section of the city. Nor is it defined by residence per se. It is a landscape defined by access and utility, by how the people who use 'Kaloleni' define it as part of the urban region of Nairobi. Luo in Nairobi define their association with Kaloleni, their belonging to Kaloleni, by the frequency of their activities there rather than by whether they reside in the community. This feature of definition, somewhat precise, somewhat ambiguous, gives Ololo, as Kaloleni is also known, its cosmopolitan character. Wider issues and attentions, rather than narrowly Kaloleni issues, are always afloat in the Kaloleni neighbourhoods, and one does not need to be settled physically within Kaloleni to gain entry to the discussions. The openness of discourse in Kaloleni gives thousands of Luo in Nairobi a feeling of being wholly a part of Kaloleni without necessarily residing there.

In the eastern part of Nairobi, in an area known as Eastlands, there is a municipal housing estate called Kaloleni. Of all such estates, it has by far the largest proportion of Luo. It is often called a Luo estate by members of all ethnic groups in the city. Luo hold almost all of their numerous ethnic association meetings there. A trusted visitor may be shown the houses used by prominent Luo politicians. Adjacent to the estate is the national sports stadium, which is mostly used for soccer matches between Luo teams and teams drawn from another ethnic group, the Luyia.[2]

This ambiguity surrounding the meaning of Kaloleni as a community underlines the force and meaning of the production of a landscape in the city. There is resonance with what we now understand are other ambiguous and working identities with 43 social and geographical space in old Siaya, where one might be known as, and feel oneself, a person of Alego or Gem or Karuchuonyo, while not residing there at all.

Ambiguous Kaloleni returns us to another issue, the multiplication of useful and intimate identifications with social space that are built and used by Luo as they move themselves around the landscapes of Siaya, western Kenya, Nairobi's urban region, and the Indian Ocean coast.

Within Kaloleni, and in contrast to the openness of the definition of Kaloleni, are the restricted and self-defining 'clubs' of specific consociation. There is the 'Asembo Republic' and the 'Seme Community'. And, in a still more restrictive sense, there is the Orindi club, a highly visible, vocal group of Gor Mahia football fans who live in the Mathare Valley area. Then there is the Nyanza Bar club, consisting of the clerical cadres who drink their beer communally in a downtown pub. There is also the 'Ugenya collective', which 'waters' at Umina Bar, also downtown.

And there is the core association formed by the Kaloleni Club, a middle-management elitist club that has redefined its form and function over the years. In the 1950s it was patronized by Argwings-Kodhek and Tom Mboya, and its major preoccupation was the development of congress-type political movements. It absorbed the political activity and football politics of the 1960s. In the 1970s it was largely an entertainment centre, with harpists as the main showpiece. And, by the early 1980s, it had changed its function yet again; it had become a discussion club, but still organized around an interest in football.

It is said that by 1965 it became public knowledge among Luo in Nairobi that the factions within the Luo Union leadership were aligned behind Odinga and Mboya. The minority pro-Mboya faction, allegedly coming mostly from South Nyanza and from Kisumu and Seme locations, wanted to change the name of the Luo Union in Nairobi to the Luo Sports Club. The minority argued that the organization's activities were recreational, i.e. soccer, as well as welfare-oriented, and that to continue with the name, Luo Union, was falsely to emphasize a 'tribalist' organization potentially in political conflict with the 'non-tribal' state of Kenya, represented by the ruling party, KANU.[3]

The interior of Kaloleni has its own social structure; there are VIPs like Aton Lubera, who is an encyclopaedia on all kinds of subjects; Osewe, the 'MD' (Managing Director), catering for the lunches of the middle classes; plus Mwenda Ball, who prides himself on being able to identify the owner of every car by its registration plate; and there are the Virunga sisters, who form a bridge between the Luo community and the Zaïrois musicians and business men passing through Nairobi.

There is also a generational, gerontological structure to Kaloleni: the Omwandas, Ofafas, Gwadas, Magungas and Ajodes of the 1940s have by the 1980s been replaced as the Kaloleni elite by their children: Crispo, Fwaya, Dave, and Baby. There are other continuities of the Kaloleni landscape. The Acacia 'drive-in' open space between the shops in Nairobi West may be regarded as an extension of Luo Kaloleni. Its emergence is due to two elements: a new football stadium, Nyayo National; and the Luo bar, the K'Odundo, operated by the family of Odundo. The issues that dominate discussion at K'Odundo are the same as those of Kaloleni: Gor Mahia and Luo Union football clubs. If continuous discourse forms parts of the wider social meaning of Kaloleni, it is football that forms the central topic positing an alternative spiritual republic: the Gor Republic as an alternative to the secular Kenya state. Discussions begun in Kaloleni before a home match at Kaloleni grounds are easily continued at K'Odundo after the game. Similarly, the details of an afternoon match held at Nyayo Stadium flow easily into conversation in the Kaloleni bars by eight o'clock in the evening. These discussions may be continued at KaAdongo Bar in Eastleigh as well. Farther afield there are well-known Luo clubs like BTM in the Athi River area to which the middle classes of Nairobi drive every weekend for Zaïrois music; the Bristol Club in Mombasa; and Kinda Club in Nakuru.

In late 1965, Luo Sports Club and Kisumu Hot Stars played at the Nairobi Stadium in a match which is still talked about today with avid enthusiasm. But the content of the talk is less to do with the soccer played than with the opportunity the match provided for a clear expression of the Odinga—Mboya split within the Luo community. Both Odinga and Mboya attended before a packed stadium. The Kisumu Hot Stars were in peak form. The two factions occupied distinct areas of the stadium, one chanting Odinga's slogans, the smaller faction chanting Mboya ... When Mboya presented ... [the Mboya] Cup to the victorious team, which was now clearly identified with his 'rival', Odinga, there was a great deal of abuse hurled at Mboya. Mboya became angry and rebuked the crowd ... Incidents followed the match, including an attempt to assault Mboya in his car as he was driven away, and numerous arrests. Among those arrested were two of the star soccer players originally poached from the Luo Union [team identified with Mboya] and on this day playing for the Kisumu Hot Stars.[4]

Boro

Boro is a little market village in western Kenya. When the old buses rumble into Boro from Kisumu, they have reached close to the end of the line. There is a sub-county administrative office in Boro, a little collection of shops selling such things as soap, parts for lamps and kerosene, and a postal sub-station. Side by side, there are two tiny hotels that will serve you *ugali* (steamed maizemeal), the staple food of the area. You can get *ugali* served alone, *ugali* with a fish sauce, *ugali* with a meat sauce, *ugali* with a chicken sauce. The hotels have three or four rooms, cells really, occupied occasionally by traders who come to Boro, but more actively used by the three or four prostitutes who prowl the market. There are three bars in Boro, all selling warm beer and warm soda. Many of the independent and very idiosyncratic Christian sects of western Kenya have meeting halls within shouting distance of the market. Indeed, on market days ... that is, twice a week ... you can get quite lost in the cacophony of buyers, sellers, noisy drunks, and liturgists.

There is a small mill in Boro; grinding maize, or corn, into meal for cooking. For the cost of a few matches, the miller will grind your maize and return it to you in your bag. The mill, powered by a small petrol engine, is too small to handle more than a couple of hundred kilogrammes of maize a day, and neither assists the farmers of the area to participate in the national maize market as producers nor makes it possible for the farmers of the region to be self-sufficient in food. Indeed, the survival of Boro's countryside, seemingly rich in grain, cassava, and cattle, hangs on the success of its men and women getting work in Mombasa, Nairobi, and Kisumu, and sending back remittances to their spouses, parents, siblings, and children in the countryside. Boro is one nucleus within an expansive labour reserve, a niche in a national and international economy.[5]

Most days the Boro market square has a look of desolation. The small shops on the square do little trade, the bars serve few drinks, and few folk are found in and around the churches. Those days, the square appears the property of the young 'cowboys', as Nashon, a teacher in Boro, calls the young men who hang idly about the square in fancy dress. One historian of Kenya has seen the situation of these youths as the tragic consequence of colonial and world forces leading to the decline of a once active and resilient peasantry to the state of what he takes as 'Marx's "idiocy of rural life" '.[6]

Twice a week, the market place, an enclosure the size of a football field, comes alive with people and goods. On a typical market day, one might find twenty sellers of fish, a half-dozen bicycle repairmen, forty or fifty women selling small quantities of locally grown grains, tubers, and spices. There are a dozen or so sellers of almost identical collections of cups, saucers, plates, aluminum cookware, and linens. There are a half-dozen sellers of new textiles, with the same fifteen or twenty fabrics hung here and there. The largest areas are taken up by used-clothing traders, and most of the clothing appears to be of American origin, of 1940s and 1950s vintage. There are a dozen preparers of cooked food for denizens of the market, and for a shilling or two you can have a warm meal. A few elderly ladies seek buyers for pots they have made and carried to market, but Boro is not a place to buy pots. The finer local ware is to be found at Ngiya, along the road to Kisumu, and in Kisumu itself, the region's largest town, one hundred kilometres away. Two basket sellers appear on bicycles on market days, each bike loaded with thirty or forty baskets of varying size and function, and a third basket trader — an aristocrat in the basket industry — arrives by bus with his wares. Indeed, in terms of value and volume, the greater part of the goods brought to the Boro market each market day are conveyed there by peripatetic country traders, who, it seems, must reckon the day of the week by the market they find themselves in. If it's Ngiya, it must be Wednesday.

There is a cattle pen in Boro, the scene of an occasional cattle market where large cash transactions would sometimes take place; but from late 1979 until early 1981, there was not a single cattle sale. The cattle market was invariably cancelled, just on the eve of a cattle market day, by a suspected outbreak of foot-and-mouth disease. The closure orders came down from the administrative offices close by the market. These offices include the local magistrate's court, the sub-county officer's station, with its small staff, an education office, and a police post. Perhaps seven or eight civil and police officials may be found on the rosters of Boro's administrative apparatus, but it is sometimes difficult to find the official you need. The officials are away on long and short leaves. And their constant attention at the regional offices 12km away is customary, if not required, and the routine absence of officials from Boro became part of the context of the 'Christmas revolution' in Boro in 1979 and 1980.[7]

Runaway fathers

There has been a tendency among observers of Siaya to see a critical and dynamic tension between the Siaya countryside and the opportunities and demands of the Kenya cities: Kisumu, Nairobi, and Mombasa. Yet there is another side of Siaya, almost missed in the approaches to Siaya's past and that of larger western Kenya.

Many Luo today recall the phenomenon of the 'runaway husband' or the 'runaway father', the adult male who rose one morning and disappeared from the household and from Siaya. Sometimes these sons of Siaya were never seen again. Members of deserted families listened closely to the news from Uganda for news of husband or father. Uganda was the known refuge of hundreds, perhaps thousands, of Luo men.

The Luo 'migrations' to southern Uganda — in reverse along the routes which were, young Luo learned, the heroic passageways of Luo pioneers into western Kenya three or more centuries ago — became important from the mid-1940s on. These migrations included not only the 'runaway', but also thousands of Luo men and women who sought new forms of income to remit to their households in Siaya. For the people of Siaya, southern Uganda was from the 1940s to the 1960s a very different world from that of wider Kenya. Outside the Siaya countryside, wider Kenya offered the detestable 'opportunities' of farm labour, or, alternatively, channels into low levels of teaching and clerical work in government offices and companies — all at very low wages, and with few recognized opportunities outside wage labour. Southern Uganda, by contrast, was viewed by the people of Siaya as a world wide open to freebooting enterprise and to the simultaneous integration of income from separate activities.

In Uganda, people from Siaya developed a substantial hold on what we would today call the 'informal sector': beer-brewing, renting of housing, marketing activities. They did not shirk from dirty jobs like cleaning and charcoal-burning, and came quietly and invisibly to assume the role of a dynamic immigrant population. For those of Siaya, between 1945 and 1972, Kenya offered, at best, avenues to respectability, albeit a shabby respectability, through education; Uganda offered opportunities for true accumulation. It was commonly said that when you returned home to Siaya from a period of wage labour 'in Kenya' you came home with a blanket and a gunny sack of grain, but if you came back from Uganda you came with cash and actual material wealth: bicycles, sewing machines, and taxis. An example of a returnee from Uganda is Onyango Ochang', who started off by plying the Kampala—Busia road as a taxi driver in the 1940s. Ochang' accumulated savings and by the 1970s he was the owner of a garage in Kisumu and of a fleet of buses, the Nyataya Bus Service.

In Uganda, the Luo came to see themselves as invisible men and women who could slip easily into new opportunities in farming, trading, vegetable marketing, timber, charcoal, and various services, largely remaining outside regular employment, often working at several activities at the same time. Back in Siaya, many invested this wealth earned in Uganda in housing and shops, though they learned from an early date that the returns from commerce in Siaya would never match those obtainable in much wealthier southern Uganda, where Africans had more cash, consumed more from the markets, and participated in a much higher velocity of circulation of all goods and currencies. By their Uganda experience, the men and women of Siaya understood more clearly the meanings and effects of wage labour in the Kenya colony and, later, nation.

The Siaya migrants also brought home a very distinctive knowledge of Uganda. It was not uncommon at Christmas for neighbours in Siaya to gather around one of their comrades just back on vacation from Uganda and to listen in on a penetrating analysis of political events in Uganda. Returning Luo men observed that the British and the Baganda treated them virtually as invisible beings as they performed services on behalf of the colonial officials and the new and old Ugandan leadership. But while in some respects they could feel invisible, they were not necessarily anonymous. One recalls Simeon Othieno Odiemo, who was driver to the Chief Secretary in the Uganda Protectorate Government, and Wilson Oluoch Oton, who was cook to the Governor, Sir Andrew Cohen. Later there was President Obote's driver, Ogola, who was given a state funeral when he died in 1983. Their invisibility in Uganda made it possible for them to observe private areas of the lives of administrators; these migrant Luo brought stories 'home for Christmas'.

These visits home and these stories — and the intelligence they conveyed — joined Siaya even more closely to southern Uganda. People across Siaya were able to speak with knowledge about the situations, occupations, and experiences of their countrymen in Uganda. Many Luo learned to use the Kisumu—Port Bell steamer service to great advantage, carrying small loads back and forth between Kenya and Uganda. Luo fishermen found the Uganda lakeshore hospitable to their camps and far closer to large markets than the landings in Siaya. In Uganda, Luo fishermen found they could reach markets without the intervention of middlemen. Later, Luo learned quickly the complex framework of smuggling between Siaya and Amin's Uganda (and post-Amin Uganda), which overtook all other commercial activity in which Luo from western Kenya were involved.

Outside the regular purview of the Uganda state, Luo men resettled the southern Busoga (Uganda) areas closed earlier by sleeping sickness. They reopened a productive agricultural zone and moved quickly into the production and marketing of vegetables for the towns and market centres along the Iganga—Jinja road. Indeed, they were so successful in these markets that different sections of Ugandan society eventually found them a threat to their influence in the local economy.

Some curious paradoxes developed in the households of the runaway husbands and fathers. Households that had lost their

49

male heads to Uganda were taken over by women and run for years as if the men were dead. Women like Anna Aluoch of Nyadhi, Roslida Achieng' of Liganua, and Mariana Jagam of Got Osimbo managed their households in this way for upwards of two decades. The remaining male kin of the runaway husbands gradually lost their influence over the household yet, in time, sons of the runaways considered going out in search of their fathers. Some actually travelled to Uganda, and a few even returned with their fathers, who were gradually reintegrated in the home. One of the motives behind this search was the disadvantage the sons of runaway fathers had in arranging marriages for themselves. 'Going to look for father' became a common theme along the roads from Siaya to Busia. When fathers were returned to Siaya they most often never returned to their households — wives and children — in southern Uganda; there, again, the women took up the entire management of the household, whether in town or in the reopened agricultural zones of southern Busoga.

By 1968 the Luo presence in southern Uganda was so strong, and their hold on many services and trades in the Kampala peri-urban region was so pronounced that the Uganda Government decided to expel them. Within a year or so, the Luo started trickling back from Kenya and soon their numbers were back to former levels. In 1975, they were pushed out again, not this time by government order but rather by army-instigated violence, particularly in the Jinja area and in the southern Busoga areas near the Magamaga barracks of Amin's army.

From 1975, the Uganda connection took on a new character. The collapse of administration in Uganda under Amin, and the effect of tyranny on the market, encouraged smallholding Ugandan coffee producers to sell their beans directly to Kenyan buyers waiting along the Uganda—Kenya border. While this was often referred to as smuggling, some of the highest officials in Kenya found it to be a most lucrative business proposition. The traffic along the road from Kisumu to Busia (on the Uganda border), became so busy in 'Uganda traffic' that a very considerable investment in roadside bars, hostels, and hotels was made everywhere along the coffee route. Such pleasure resorts as the Trailer Inn, Jera Inn, and the Savanna Club were built during this period. Sleepy market centres such as Jera, Sega, and Ugunja began to take on a centrality in the minds of the fast-moving clientele as places to eat, to entertain and to close deals. The artery from Kisumu to Busia became known popularly as the 'Ugenya Riviera'.

Nashon's journey

Boro lies about forty kilometres from the Uganda border, and the topic of Uganda was a familiar aspect of conversations among the young in Boro. In one sense, this was a very old discourse, for the Luo-speaking people of western Kenya share a very deep history with people across much of eastern and northern Uganda, many western Kenyans migrated to Uganda for employment and for new agricultural opportunities in the colonial period, and some of the brightest of western Kenyans acquired their highest education at Makerere College (later Makerere University College and Makerere University) in Kampala. But these conversations every evening in Boro had a new edge, and this was the story of smuggling (*magendo*); the risks, opportunities, the big winners, and the big losers, how to get in, how to get out, and so forth. Significantly, none of the young of Boro had themselves participated in the Uganda smuggling operations, and none knew well anyone who had participated. But they were full of information — well, rumours — about this person or that person who had made a big hit or taken a big loss. Stories of upward mobility in wider Kenya, as they were told in Boro, nearly always had a *magendo* component. Expensive cars, high political office, and new houses or businesses were, in the Boro conversations, financed out of *magendo*.

Early in 1980, Nashon's teaching post was redefined and his salary was changed. Nashon was not surprised when his pay failed to come through for one month, then two months, then three. He began to make inquiries, first at the administrative offices across the road from the Boro archaeological camp, then at Siaya, then Kisumu, and he even travelled to Nairobi. He began to be short in the pocket, even though his friends helped him as much as they could. He needed some quick cash and found someone with a big car in Siaya who promised to take him on an expedition to Uganda. The procurer needed an aide for one journey, and indicated to Nashon that he could make a quick bundle. Nashon would be collected in front of the Boro administrative offices at 11pm that night.

A somewhat frightened Nashon turned up at the Boro archaeological camp around dusk. There was a good deal of questioning, and Nashon revealed all he knew about the planned operation, which was not very much. There was a considerable needling, some of it pretty scary, concerning what would happen if Nashon were picked up by the Uganda police or army or thieves or dissidents, or just abandoned somewhere in Uganda

51

by his patron. That evening in Boro, most of the young hanging about the camp were dubious about whether Nashon's journey to Uganda would come off; either Nashon would not have the courage or his patron would not turn up. The anticipation, the doubt, provided a context for a long and deep discussion of the industry of Ugandan smuggling.

Since 1977 there had been constant talk among the young about stereos, televisions, BMWs, outboard motors, tea, and coffee being purchasable in Uganda at low prices in Kenya shillings. The Kenya shilling was at this time not readily convertible, but for many Ugandans the Kenya shilling promised salvation from a collapsing Uganda currency. It was remarked that many of the treasured goods smuggled into Kenya were either re-exported (as in the case of tea and coffee) or resold as consumer goods within Kenya. Thousands of people were involved in the traffic, according to the stories that evening, but only a very small crowd were making fortunes from the traffic. The agricultural boom in Kenya in the late 1970s was said by the young to be much assisted by the inclusion of a good deal of the output of Uganda, Rwanda, and Zaïre in Kenya exports, to the profit of Kenyan millionaires and officials who bought agricultural commodities for low prices and then resold them through Kenyan channels where higher prices were obtainable. There was much discussion of the success of one Kenya minister of state, whom the young called 'Dr Magendo', a figure who participated brilliantly in this traffic.

Among the young in Boro, it was believed that many of the goods smuggled over the Kenya border reached Uganda (by air or, ironically, by transit across Kenya) free of duty, imported into Uganda by high-ranking officials and diplomats. Some of the young speculated that a good part of the goods brought over into Kenya, including expensive cars, had been stolen from individuals in Kenya, the thieves then seeking refuge in Uganda. Ten years earlier, a similar pattern of transport of stolen goods had moved valuable merchandise and vehicles into Zaïre.

With the high Ugandan demand for Kenya shillings (indeed, for liquidity of any kind) and the very imperfect collection of duties by the Uganda government, 'Ugandan' goods could be obtained at a very low price in western Kenya. For example, smuggled kerosene and petroleum sold in half litre bottles in and around Boro at a much lower price than bulk kerosene and petroleum sold at petrol stations. In 1980, it was cheaper in western Kenya to buy petrol by the 'pint' than by the 'gallon'. This perhaps partly explained why petrol was in such short supply in Uganda or was constantly 'disappearing from the market'.

The young of Boro speculated about whether the western Kenyan market for cheap petrol had disabled President Amin's motorized divisions in 1979, contributing decisively to Amin's downfall. The young also spoke with evident expertise on the 'bottle trade', which involved profiteering on the disappearance of beer and soft-drink bottles from Uganda, a phenomenon that was disabling Ugandan breweries and bottlers. The young observed that the smuggling of bottles into Uganda had become profitable and was in turn creating shortages in Kenya. Ugandans were, it was argued, finding it more profitable to bottle kerosene and petrol than beer. Uganda beer could only be sold for Uganda shillings, while 'Uganda' petrol yielded foreign exchange.

It was the 'bottle trade' that Nashon's patron was involved in, at least on this occasion. As Nashon waited at the administrative offices that night, he heard a car coming up the Siaya road crashing along, not quite the quiet conveyance that he and the rest of us had assumed a smuggler would need. The car was full of bottles. Nashon climbed in and they jangled across the Uganda border sometime in the middle of the night. Thirty kilometres or so into Uganda, the car turned off a main road and the patron asked Nashon to get out and wait along the road. He told Nashon that he did not want him to see the Ugandan contact. A very anxious Nashon climbed out of the car. Two hours later, the patron returned, collected Nashon, and they returned across the border to Kenya, where Nashon received a one-hundred shilling note for his effort but not a word on the reason for, or value of, his participation. All he knew was that the car had been full of pillows, linen bedsheets, and embroidered bedspreads when he was dropped off in Boro. While the young of Boro 'knew' the smuggling industry in terms of complex currency transfers, poor Nashon had to relate that there was probably no cash exchange involved in this particular transaction; it appeared to be a barter deal. And while a rich knowledge and considerable authority seemed to punctuate the discussions of these young who had never participated directly or indirectly in smuggling, and a powerful political sociology was evolved around the discussion of this topic, the participant Nashon was, paradoxically, left completely in the dark about what had happened on his 'Uganda journey'.

Sweet properties

The 'Kenyatta Bequest' opened up a new homeland for Luo settlement in the sugar belt also known as Muthaiga. With independence, large sections of land in the European highlands 53 of Kenya became available for resettlement by Africans. Beginning in 1964, Luo began to purchase parcels of between 10 acres (4 ha) and 2,000 acres (800 ha) in the new settlement scheme in the former European area of the Kisumu-Londiani District, extending 100km from Kibos to the Tinderet Hills. If you had one-thousand to eight-thousand shillings, and the knowledge of how to go about acquiring freeholds, a new world was opened to you. The intention of the Kenya state was to establish capitalist farmers on their own lands. Within a few years, two thousand Luo had acquired parcels in this new homeland, ranging from Dr Onyango-Abuje's 10 acres to Mrs Abura's 2,000 acres. A similar process of 'new settlement' was organized in the Lambwe Valley of South Nyanza. The new homeland east of Kisumu extended from the edges of the Indian sugar belt into the hills of Tinderet about Fort Ternan, including lands that had been producing sugar for some decades as well as virgin land.

The list of early Luo 'settlers' in the new homeland reads like a list of the Luo elite of Kenya, composed mainly of senior civil servants and professionals, who were finding in the new homeland opportunities for investment of savings from their employment and professions. Sociologically, the settlement of the 'new homeland' by Luo is replete with paradoxical elements demanding further study. Luo saw the new homeland as allowing them to build new homes away from both the turbulence of the city and the rural poverty of Siaya and other areas of western Kenya. More importantly, many Luo saw an opportunity to establish a degree of distance from what has been referred to by the philosopher Dr D.A. Masolo as 'the incessant Luo anthropology': the unceasing claims on their accumulations from relatives for money, hospitality, helping with bridewealth, funeral expenses, and job seeking.

The sugar belt lands were quickly seen as a safe haven for accumulations produced by better-paid occupations and professions. These investments in the countryside constituted a sharp departure in the lives of the emerging Luo elite. The character of growth of a Luo elite in twentieth-century Kenya, and particularly in Nairobi, was marked by a credo of deprivation: on the one hand, the rural world, including Siaya, offered no opportunities for the forward-looking Luo, indeed the countryside had an impoverishing effect with its limited production and immense claims upon savings; on the other hand, so the credo avers, outside of the Luo reserves, including Siaya, the Kikuyu have privileged access to all resources.

This credo, this view of independent Kenya, whatever its truth, was broadly accepted among Luo. Consequently they defined their new world, the arena in which their opportunities would lie, in slowly moving forward in a growing number of occupations and professions in urban areas, and in a kind of low-voiced ethnic struggle against the perceived Gikuyu hegemony. So taking up the opportunities for freehold in the new settlement scheme seemed to portend a great change in the working values of the elite.

Yet, the new Luo proprietors have continued to operate with the essential credo in mind. They have remained in Nairobi, in their professions and occupations, pushing forward there and pushing against what they sometimes remark is Gikuyu predominance in Kenyan society. The effect is that men and women in their forties and fifties, resident in Nairobi, have been going into full-scale agriculture in a part-time way, with minimal knowledge of the management skills of farming on this scale. While it is often voiced that 'the Kenyatta Bequest' has allowed Luo to put sugar on their land 'by telephone from Nairobi', what the proprietors usually find is that the telephone brings them news that planting, cutting, transport and the work force on their lands are badly disarranged. Many have come to see the absentee farm as unlikely to succeed, but the farm remains for most the avocation, and in some senses is being transferred slowly from fully productive land, to a reserve for precious capital, to new status, and to a new locus for living.

In time, some of the more elderly civil servants among the proprietors have been retiring to the new homeland. Some of the landholders who have been troubled by the difficulties of production, seeing the weaknesses imparted by absentee ownership, have sent their children to agricultural colleges. Others make do by visiting at weekends. Two decades of Luo proprietorship in the new homeland of the sugar belt and Tinderet have now passed, and one is beginning to see some of the effects of the Luo 'migrations' into this new terrain.

It is clear that the injection of capital into the purchase and operation of the new farms has slowed the return of capital and income to old Siaya. Additionally, a division has been opened between the proprietary part-time farmers in the sugar belt and the small farmers whose families have been in the area for a generation or more. The Kano smallholders in the former African reserves were expected to participate fully in a system of sugar outgrowing. Once optimistic farmers, they feel bypassed on their one-acre and two-acre holdings. At times the smallholders have felt terrible effects from a full abandonment of food production for sugar. The stratification of the sizes of farm parcels has produced what appear to be significant feelings of class conflict within small communities between those Luo owning 2000 acres and those holding only two or ten. Many Luo see these tensions as the first such abrasions that have been experienced by their people.

The new sugar belt investments have placed urban Luo from Nairobi, often politically progressive, in an ambiguous position in relation to the issues of estate labour and union organization in the sugar belt. It is the 'unanticipated dimension': the break between capital and labour in the 'New Homeland'. In spite of the disappointments and new anxieties, some Luo now see that they can produce for themselves more luxurious lives in the 'new Luo homeland', located as it is at a distance both from the high costs of goods, services, and housing in the city, and also from the never ceasing demands of relations for payments for schooling, marriages, funerals, and investments. Hundreds of well-heeled Luo therefore leave Nairobi on Friday afternoons for their farms, where they preside on Saturdays and Sundays, thus weakening their associational life in the city. The traverse from city and farm is a hazardous one in many respects, not least of which is the high rate of road fatalities along this very route, leaving a startling number of widows and dependants trying to hold together the triangular arrangements of Siaya, the city, and the sugar belt.

The difficulties of small-scale growers and private farmers, now greatly enlarged by the participation of privateers in the sugar belt and Tinderet Hills, tend to be deflected toward and against Indians, who control the largest sugar estate — the Miwani nuclear estate and factory. And, while the increased participation of Luo in private farming has intensified discussion of difficulties in private sector farming in Kenya (labour, transport, markets, credit, absentee management), the Kenya government, large private capital, and international organizations chose to read the enthusiasm for the 'new Luo homeland' as evidence of a transformation of the western Kenya economy — a great new sugar frontier. Consequently, they constructed a gigantic molasses plant, the largest capital investment ever in western Kenya. This plant did not take off and is expected to produce no significant amount of molasses (whether for Kenyan use or for export). It is now widely remarked in western Kenya that the plant has managed to generate a very substantial export after all: that is the export from Kenya of debt service payments on the capital borrowed for construction.

'Build yourself a house'

In the 1950s and the 1960s Luo urban workers (the *Jopango*) were well known for not having satisfactory houses in the rural countryside and were teased because of this. It was well understood that the *simba* (bachelor's hut) could fall down as a consequence of not being used for long periods of time. A song was sung that played both on the separation from the countryside and the abandonment of the valued *simba*, while perhaps remarking on the labour force emerging in Nairobi.

> Biye onwangó
> Od Japango
> Biye tengó ten'g!

> (The white ants have discovered
> The worker's hut.
> How they mince it!)

The issue of separation from the countryside became more prominent in the 1960s. It was a period of clearly perceptible upward mobility: a great number of people from Siaya were benefiting from the Africanization policies of the Kenya government and were then joining the category of 'big' people. Those around these emerging 'big' people in Nairobi held them accountable for their failure to establish some permanent home in the Luo reserves, a place to return to at retirement, or at vacations, a ground to be buried in.

The automobile produced a second intervention, but not only because it provided individuals with a ready means of connecting their homes in Nairobi and Mombasa with their *simbas* in the Siaya countryside. Motorists died on the highways in great numbers and the Luo settled in the urban areas applied great pressure to promote Siaya burial — that those who died 'outside' must be brought home for burial. Oginga Odinga once remarked that the Siaya country burial of deceased urban Luo was an outcome of the growth of Luo affluence in the 1950s and 1960s. Before this, from the 1920s to the 1940s, according to Odinga, those who died away from Nyanza were buried wherever they had passed away.

When a body was returned to the countryside and a funeral celebrated at the *simba* of the deceased, the condition of the 'country estate' was noted by those who attended, as if it summarized the deceased's whole life. In funeral after funeral, observations were made about the poor, decrepit situation in the countryside

compared with the fairly substantial housing that the deceased
had occupied in the city. Feelings of shame and embarrassment
visited all these funerals and gave pause to many of the celebrants,
causing them to consider investing funds in the improvement
of the *simba*. The harpist Apuot Ochieng' distilled these feelings
in a song that is recognized as one of the most poignant verses
to circulate since the early 1960s:

> Gero gae odi
> Kata otin
> Gero gae odi
> Kata otin
> Masira Jamuomre
> Tho onyuolo yuak
> Inyalo Kunyi
> To ikunyo ot

> (Build yourself a house
> Even a small one
> Build yourself a house
> Even a small one
> Accidents don't warn
> Death capitulates mourning.
> It's no good our digging your grave
> As well as your house's foundation.)

Luo in Siaya and Nairobi today attribute to Apuot and his
songs the expression that pressed many Luo to pay attention
to the condition of their rural homes, to the extent that by 1984,
Awiti Osendo, an eminent Luo architect, observed that every up-
and-coming Luo elite member encountered in Siaya, Homa Bay,
or Kisumu on weekends would be talking about the houses they
were building at home. Indeed, the investment in the enhanced
simba became a new and primary symbol of 'making it' in the
swirl of politics, business, society, and, of course, funerals. The
continuous discussion of the quality of houses in the countryside
— the virtues of a well-built *simba* — has been, and remains,
a powerful connection among the several landscapes of Siaya.

A comprehension of 'Siaya' involves attempting to gain conceptual control of the simultaneous production of the several
Siaya landscapes from Kampala to Mombasa, and beyond.
Where do we locate our analytical boundaries? How do we see
the parts and the wholes of our Siaya? How do we view the
aggregation of atomistic constructions of identity and knowledge,
and the mobilization of intimate concerns? And how do we link

an interest in the more general social processes and structures to observations of transient local conditions and personal material situations such as the fainting of the child Obalo in 1980 discussed in the next chapter?

NOTES

1. Meja Mwangi, *Going Down River Road* (London, Heinemann, 1976), p. 179.
2. David Parkin, *The Cultural Definition of Political Response* (London, Academic Press, 1978), p. 36. Parkin offers an extended study of the social organization of Kaloleni.
3. ibid., p. 221.
4. ibid., p. 223
5. This description of Boro is drawn from David William Cohen, 'Christmas discos and other things: the discourse of the dominated in a Kenyan village', a paper presented to the 4th International Roundtable in Anthropology and History, Bad Homburg, West Germany, October 1983. In 1978, Grace and Allan Ogot suggested to David William Cohen that he open research on several sites within the area of Alego in western Kenya. The focus of Cohen's research in Siaya was the pre-colonial past, but at the same time he made notes of observations made 'out of the corner of the eye'. These were later developed into a series of Boro stories.
6. E.S. Atieno Odhiambo, 'The rise and fall of the Kenya peasant, 1888-1922', in Peter C. W. Gutkind and Peter Waterman, (eds), *African Social Studies: A Radical Reader* (London, Heinemann, 1977), p. 240.
7. See Chapter 6 below.

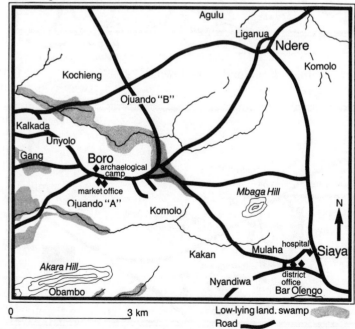

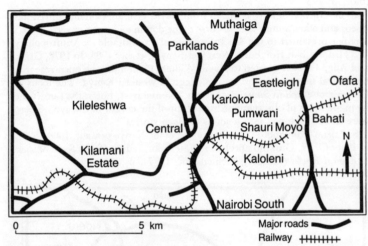

Map 4: Boro, Liganua and Siaya town
Map 5: Boro

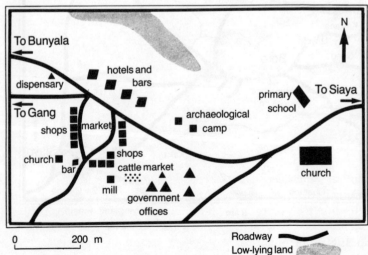

The Hunger of   IV
Obalo

Idongo Ka wod jo Machon.

He is fully grown like people of long ago.[1]

In 1980, a child, Obalo, fainted in Liganua. There was immediate crying and shrieking. People in the neighbourhood of the child's home rushed to see what was happening. Those present did not know what to do, though there was general agreement that the child had fainted from hunger. They did not know, they did not remember, how to revive a child who had fainted from hunger. This was a period when hunger was familiar, and such periods of hunger — seeing, being with hungry people, being hungry oneself — were common enough, but the further effect of a child fainting was not within the recollected experience of those present.

Siaya District, in the twentieth century, is not a region that could be described as an ecological disaster zone. Siaya has experienced drought, but it cannot be characterized as an area likely to experience severe drought or famine over long periods. Yet it is an area that has experienced hunger in the twentieth century; and currently hunger is present over much of Siaya for weeks and months every year. Today, it is commonly understood that two years out of every five or seven will be poor in rain, resulting in severe food shortages.

Hunger in Siaya has a distinctive history as a motor of social change. It is selective in its effects; it connects national and international forces and conditions to the adequacies and inadequacies of food available to the household; it extends and reproduces itself through the way people of Siaya participate in labour and commodity markets; it marks gender relations and gives physical meaning to distinctions between male and female activity; it centres itself in the planning of household activity; it transforms the social relations of household members into or toward money exchange relations; it conveys its effects to the children of the   *61* next generation, in their physical and mental health; and it leads to the formation of internally realized constructs of the state. The story of Obalo brings attention to the uneven way in which hunger is experienced in Siaya. In periods of serious drought in Siaya, children and cattle are most affected by the extended periods of food shortages and the disappearance of fodder. At other times there are seasonal shortages of food, and hunger is experienced towards the end of the long dry season and through the beginning of the summer rains. Shortfalls in food stocks develop for several reasons. These include the exhaustion of stores of food from the previous harvest; the diminution of remittances sent by Siaya men (and occasionally also women) working outside the region, who themselves may be facing a loss of buying power in the same period; and short supplies resulting from an effort to accumulate cash for food and other purchases through the sale of 'surplus' grains during good growing seasons.

In the case of sales of 'surpluses', monetarization and the market offer the Siaya individual a means of escaping hunger while simultaneously threatening greater vulnerability. Women producers may sell grain in the market as bags of unmilled kernel to get cash to purchase other foodstuffs and other goods, and to offset short remittances from a husband or son or daughter working away from home. However, their sales come at a time when there is considerable grain available and prices are therefore low for the producer or the seller. Savings held over for periods of food risk may subsequently find foodstuffs in the market, but this will be at a time of generalized shortages when prices are high. Or grain may not be available from the market at any price. Under these circumstances some traders buy up grain during the harvest and speculatively hold it. However, from what we know of this speculation, it is on a very small scale. The shortages of cash in the countryside provide but a weak incentive to petty commodity brokers to assume considerable additional risks in storing grain in, or moving grain into, the Siaya countryside. Indeed, there has been and continues to be a tendency in commodity and livestock trade in Siaya for the trader or 'hoarder' to unload risks, and thereby stock, as quickly as possible. This tends to undermine accumulative strategies that could be characterized as gross speculation on hunger.

I was with Omuodo [Alogo, head of the family] during the 1918-19 famine called the *Kanga*, and I have never forgotten his actions. He would fetch me late every night and take me from granary to granary to examine the food stocks. When we found a granary with little left in it he would direct me to a granary which had plenty, and we would replenish the almost exhausted store. When I asked why he did this he said we should be kind to those who had nothing. Women with many children had greater need, and to prevent argument over food shares, he thought it best to arrange a re-distribution himself, by night.[2]

There is considerable popular expression of the view that food shortages are worsened by those associated with the grain markets: in the Ministry of Agriculture, among the big international traders, and those regulating the national grain market. In fact, government and parastatal policies severely limit the movement of surplus grain from one district to another outside the grain board system. These policies, which are an inheritance from colonial days, sometimes allow surpluses in excess of grain board demand to rot in the fields of nearby Kakamega while Siaya experiences shortfalls in its supplies. Permits are only very rarely issued to maize traders to allow them to transport grain between Bungoma and Siaya. In respect to grain, eastern Kakamega and nearby Siaya are effectively on different sides of the globe.

In Siaya, there has been little broad and demonstrative response to the rather widely spread phenomena of shortages and hunger. The common response to such hunger in Siaya has been, and is, simply to try to live through these periods of hunger, to hope that the short rainy season will improve the food stocks available to the household and that additional funds will be remitted to the households from outside Siaya. It is a given that food production and the food market in Siaya are fragile elements. Women and children resident in the countryside absorb the effects of this fragile situation, as they experience shortages in available grains and other foodstuffs and shortages of cash for going into the market to satisfy hunger. Arguably, the shortages in the countryside are, and have been, especially cruel to children and women, producing anxieties and actual nutritional deficits.

People in Siaya speak of the experience of continuing hunger — in which the shortages in the dry season following a poor harvest are intensified by a poor growing season or seasons which may follow — as 'dying', a condition in which considerable weight loss and debilitation are felt and are visible. And many people have come to feel that Siaya is at the threshold of a dark era in terms of the production of food.

Undoubtedly, the regularly experienced hunger in Siaya has reinvigorated the gathering economy in the countryside, in which the grain diet is supplemented so far as possible by the collection of wild vegetables, seeds, and small animals and insects. But even this response has been made problematic by the exhaustion of forest and woodland resources and by the reorganization of the Siaya landscape in the nineteenth and twentieth centuries towards monotonous or repetitive production 'strategies' that

63

offer little protection of older optimal planting zones and reserve areas. These processes have conspired to reduce the variety and also the quality of cultivated and gathered foodstuffs. Likewise, the resource base for the gathering of seasonings and medicines has also diminished.

The people of Siaya have a long-range perspective on their nutrition. It is commonly remarked that there has been a deterioration in the quality of diet in the last eighty years, a deterioration directly reflected in their observations of the diminution in physical stature of men and women. The ideal Luo stature — tall and well-built — is often looked back to, in comments upon an exceptionally sturdy young individual, 'Idongo ka wod jo Machon' ('Fully grown like the people of long ago').

'Maize means hunger'

The introduction of maize into the texture of Siaya life has been an ambiguous process. In the twentieth century, the consumption of white maize meal has been associated in Siaya with the process referred to as 'Westernization'. Maize first entered the local economy through the intervention of the colonial government, an intervention that involved pressure. Maize meal was consequently first referred to as *kuon ongere*, the white man's *ugali* or white man's food. Those who went to school (*josomo*) planted maize almost as if it were part of their given curriculum. They valorized maize, identified with the esteem that they associated with it, and so maize acquired another identity: as *kuon jonanga*, the *ugali* of the 'clothed' people. So, by a combination of pressure from colonial authorities and their agents in Siaya, and an appropriation of special value to it by those first coming to see themselves as a new elite, maize gradually seeped more broadly into the diet and the production of the people.

Because the incorporation of maize into Siaya may be associated with a variety of specific and conflictual forces — the civil authorities' demands, its role as a status symbol of local elites, at times its importance as the cash crop of the region, as well as its identification with the 'rotten' foodstuff distributed by the Kenya Farmers' Association during food shortfalls, such as in 1953 — maize stands apart from the other introduced food crops, which are regarded today as having spread imperceptibly, without perturbance, across the African terrain. For people of Siaya, maize is both a part of what is viewed as 'progress' and a part of what they term 'disaster'.

In many areas the adoption of maize as a crop also involved a new cultivation practice: planting in rows, with a second weeding to remove the undergrowth. Such cultivation practices would ensure relatively high yields per hectare, and these would be perceived as giving maize an advantage over other grains. For the laterite soils of upper Siaya, however, these practices were also a cause of soil erosion, which by the 1930s was acknowledged as the scourge of the countryside. Elsewhere in the lakeshore areas, the loamy soils could not survive the waterlogging and stagnation. The result was the continuous disguised famine that has plagued Uyoma and lower Asembo people for decades.

The place of sorghum in the ancestral Lwo economy is obscure, because, while it is distinctly subsidiary to eleusine in the Central Lwo areas, the relative importance of the two crops is reversed among the Kenya Lwo. It seems likely that this pattern primarily reflects the capabilities of the crops, however, for unlike eleusine and sesame, sorghum is a very adaptable plant. Thus, some strains can provide a creditable harvest in areas that average less than 35 inches of rain, others produce in swampy terrain, and all grow reasonably well in soils that are only moderately fertile.[3]

Within the households it has long been recognized that whatever the claims for maize, the actual yields per hectare relative to sorghum and millet on a cultivated plot are not in fact superior, particularly when nutritional value is taken into account. In terms of consumption quantities, people of Siaya recall that a harvest of maize cannot extend much further into the next harvest season than would a harvest of sorghum; hence the Ugenya cognition that maize is *lam* — light and nondurable as compared with sorghum.[4] Mothers in Siaya have long recognized that maize is inferior in nutritional value to the local sorghum and millets, and they have noticed the high incidence of kwashiorkor among children fed maize meal *uji* (porridge) at the instigation of the 'modernizing' or 'progressive' influences.

Despite this evidence, for eight decades now, the official voice has not relented in its sponsorship of maize as the preferred food crop in Siaya. In the 1960s there was even a further push to evolve new varieties of maize for the western Kenya region. Only since the 1970s has research been deployed toward evolving new varieties of the self-vindicating crop, sorghum. Significantly — and we do not know why — research on the most nutritious of the three crops, finger millet, is also at an elementary stage. For the authorities, maize has virtues as a national grain, as a potential export crop, and as an agent of the commodification of agriculture and the expansion of a regulated cash economy into the countryside. But for recent and present Siaya, maize means hunger.[5]

The *gorogoro* economy

The short rains had failed at the end of 1983, and so by February 1984 many women had no food in their granaries. It was a particularly bad year for Lewnida. In January, she had successfully delivered her ninth child, but that had left her sickly for a long time. There was no food in her granary and Lewnida had six school-going children to feed every day. She kept writing to her husband, a carpenter in the Mathare Valley, Nairobi, but the beginning of the year is a bad season for the self-employed, so he had no money to send. Lewnida tried out her alternatives: she sent out her children to eat in the neighbouring homesteads. And then she got very sick and had to borrow 50 shillings from church funds for travel to Siaya, and for food. Early in April the husband wrote, enclosing 30 shillings as his contribution. On seeing the contents of the envelope, Lewnida wept.

The literature on underdevelopment in Kenya is replete with statements to the effect that rural households subsidized urban workers by remitting foodstuffs to the towns, thereby enabling capitalists to keep African wages low for as long as possible. The quantities of such foodstuffs have never been calculated, but an observer on the Kisumu—Nairobi Road throughout the 1950s and early 1960s could not have failed but to notice the sewn *kikapu* (basket), filled with maize meal, dried fish, meat, and chicken that the passengers dragged with them. The return journey from Nairobi or Mombasa witnessed the *kikapu*'s shuttle back to Siaya, this time filled with sugar, salt, tea, bread, condensed milk, and corned beef. In addition, the workers either sent emissaries with money, or used the postal services to send money to their spouses or kin. Recent commentary suggests that this shuttle service is no longer in operation. It is argued by many housewives in Boro that they no longer have surpluses of maize meal or sorghum, and no money to buy either fish or chicken to send to their working people. Rather, what is vocalized is the extent to which the rural household has become dependent on cash remittances from working kin to subsidize subsistence at home.

A woman boards the train for Kisumu after spending six months with her husband, a Luo worker in Nairobi. The train whistle blows, the signals turn red, people are jostling on the platform, saying goodbye. The train slowly pulls out of the station. Then, the husband breaks out of the platform crowd and begins racing the train down the track. In a couple of minutes he catches up with it and yells to his wife: 'There is something important I forgot to say. Remember to weed our cassava plot!'[6]

The argument that the Siaya countryside has become unable to support itself is put forward by many women who command their households: 'The soil is tired,' they say, and this has been confirmed by the research of John Oucho and Mohammed Mukras. These researchers found that the remittances from wage labour have become the critical variable in rural survival, especially during periods of drought and shortfall. The extra burdens — such as funerals, sickness, and school fees — only serve to exacerbate this dependency. The dilemma of the husbands emerges from their study too; it is the low-paid who can least afford to remit from their salaries that are under most pressure to do so, as it is they who are most likely to have left their families in the countryside. And even among the middle classes, it is not unusual to hear stories at Boro of : 'So-and-so does not come home any more. He has abandoned his parents.'

The pay packet retains number one position in the popularity chart of any construction site... Ragged and dusty, they shove and jostle while the queue crawls almost imperceptibly towards the office pigeon hole. They receive their envelopes, rip them open and count two, three times before they are quite satisfied. Then they stuff the hard-earned, long-overdue cash into their ragged clothes; a labourer's outfit may be as emaciated as his body but the pockets are as leak-proof as his stomach. He cannot afford to lose anything.[7]

In the case of Lewnida, all she could do was cry. But then she had to somehow 'live' on the 30 shillings. What has become known as 'the shilling economy' has taken deep root in the countryside as these women struggle to stretch their remittances to the limit. The value and quantity of goods purchased by an individual woman at Kodiere market can be quite limited: a half litre of kerosene, a box of matches, a slice of Nile perch for five shillings, a quarter kilogramme of sugar, siftings of tea leaves — all this exhausts her 30 shillings. This produces a critical moment. She has yet to buy the staple, maize meal. The sellers of maize meal have steadily reduced the size of the standard measuring tin from two litres to one litre to half a litre, yet all the time the unit of measure is referred to as *gorogoro*. It is the price of the *gorogoro* that has tended to remain constant over the last one and a half decades while the measure has shrunk. The *gorogoro* economy illustrates the diminution of the household's capacity to reproduce itself at acceptable levels of subsistence in Siaya. Members of the elite, when driving from Nairobi to Uyoma, make a point of not stopping at the markets nearest to their homes. Begging by women, directly or through joking relationships, is no longer a hidden activity at these markets. Here, the differentiation of wealth becomes palpable, and expressive.

The intensification of the *gorogoro* economy has been accompanied by changes in the production of meals and in the nature

67

of sociability in households around the serving of food. In the rural household the meal has come closer to being a ration than a feast; indeed, a woman in the countryside may be preparing food in a way similar to that of her husband away at work when he prepares his evening meal. Hunger in Siaya also means that the mid-day repast disappears from the daily regimen, much as the inflation of food costs has eliminated the mid-day meal from the regimen of the low-paid worker in Nairobi. Elaborate and collective preparations of meals are reserved for funerals and political banquets. At times when the grain stores are low, food may be prepared and served quickly soon after dawn and at dusk to avoid the embarrassment of not being able to offer hospitality to kin and friends passing by the home. Some people in Siaya remember their mothers preparing and serving meals at night as a way of conserving scarce supplies during times of famine.

The paradox of abundance

European travellers — Speke, Stanley, Decken, Peters, Lugard, Johnston, Baumann, Portal — who visited the Lake Victoria region of eastern Africa in the last quarter of the nineteenth century formed images of lands of great fertility, of unending abundance, of plentiful food stocks, and of nutritional self-sufficiency. Here and there they did observe desolation, misery and famine, but these conditions were uniformly attributed to the ravages upon a fertile plain of the persisting slave trade. Through their journals, narratives, and correspondence, they transferred to Europe a picture of an African world generously endowed by nature with a salubrious economic base. They regarded the great kingdoms of the region as being a direct and positive consequence of this rich endowment. They saw great opportunities for imperial or colonial organization of tropical production of a wide range of commodities for the world market. It was man, the slave-trader, who could destroy that base. It was man, the missionary, the colonial official, who could convert this endowment to vast production for the economies of Europe and America. From their reports, great interest was excited in Europe concerning the potentialities of production and markets in the interior of eastern Africa.[8]

The European visitor was not alone in developing and communicating these portraits of abundance in eastern Africa in the late nineteenth century. Some Africans today look back to an era of prosperity at the eve of, and in the early years of, the colonial period, and they draw sharp contrasts with the eras of hardship that they have witnessed in their own mature lifetimes. Like their European visitors, they sustain these images of plenty and prosperity even as they recall the great epidemics and crises of hunger that destroyed the lives of millions in the region between 1870 and 1910, the period of installation of the new colonial regimes.

Just as there were observations in the late nineteenth century of great abundance in the areas east of Lake Victoria, so there is also evidence from before the colonial period of areas experiencing exceptional shortfalls in food production, both at the beginning of the wet season and during years of poor harvests. In western Kenya, a pattern of food exchange has been observed that had the effect of softening periodic environmental crises. This involved the opening of occasional markets in times of crisis.[9]

Oral sources record the existence in the nineteenth century of a series of market places in the interstices between drier and moister lands extending in a quarter-circle from the Winam Gulf of western Kenya to the Nile River in Uganda, and beyond.[10] From the Winam Gulf north and west to south-eastern Busoga, the drier lands lie within the circle, while the moister lands lie to the north and north-east. As one moves around the quarter-circle from Busoga toward the Winam Gulf, one finds the appearance, in times of crisis, of occasional markets organized for the exchange of livestock, grain, fish, greens, and manufactured goods. These exchanges were regulated by members of the dominant lineage in the area of the market site (and by the early years of the twentieth century, these individuals resembled the so-called 'big men' or 'almost chiefs' who are familiar to students of Africa).

In the mid-1890s, Ogalo — the market master — died and his son Ondik moved the market to its present site, nearer his own homestead. Kondik market — 'the market at Ondik's place' — thus integrated the two segments of the north—south trade and provided a common meeting-ground which remained the most important market place in Seme for some twenty years.[11]

There were important variations in production and in the frequency and nature of food crises along this continuum from the Winam Gulf to the Nile. As one moves west around the quarter circle toward the Nile one would observe a series of capitals of small pre-colonial states across Busoga that appear to have been involved actively in interzonal exchange of foodstuffs and manufactures. With some imagination, one can follow the circle west beyond the Nile and across southern and central Buganda and find along this hypothetical path both the principal capitals of the Buganda kingdom and evidence for the rudiments of an argument concerning the importance of interzonal exchange in the rise of the 'interlacustrine state'.

Moving in the other direction, that is toward the Winam Gulf area, shortages of staple foods were frequent, particularly in the lake-littoral lands affected by a more unimodal pattern of rainfall and a fairly extended dry season. From at least the eighteenth century, the lakeshore populations slowly and steadily moved upland into the more secure and productive bimodal-rainfall areas, constrained only by, first, those groups who already occupied the higher ground; second, those groups who regularly raided the higher lands from the east; and third, insufficient organization or clout to force open a wedge of land in the higher areas. This population shift toward the higher and more productive lands continues today.

To define the character and significance of this population movement in somewhat simple terms, one might suggest that the shift has meant, first, the expansion of Luo speech communities and the assimilation or integration of non-Luo-speakers into these communities (largely through marriage); second, transitions in production and diet among the populations pushing their settlements into the uplands; and, third, the compression of population in the uplands zone (yielding some of the highest rates of rural population density in twentieth-century Africa) and the beginnings of extreme soil exhaustion and woodland depletion so evident in the upland region today.[12]

The presentation of these images of great wealth, abundant resources, and tremendous promise in the Lake Victoria region in the second half of the nineteenth century is in remarkable contrast to the images of the region today presented both by its natives and by outsiders: a region affected by shortages of basic foodstuffs, great losses of productivity, immense refugee problems, hunger, disease, the disappearance of effective administration, and the collapse of transport.

The conjuncture of images of late nineteenth-century abundance and late twentieth-century poverty demands an explanation of the changes as well as a solution for the plight of millions caught within the grasp of poverty and hunger. The historical explanations of this process of impoverishment of a large region of Africa are varied. Some stress climatic and environmental deterioration. Others emphasize political disarray and war as causes of the decline of production. But most explanations share a common view of the longer historical process of production in the region.

This most common view of the history of production in the region holds to a 'subsistence to commercial farming' process of economic change in the whole region over the past century. While there are problems associated with the application of a concept of subsistence to areas producing regular and irregular surpluses for exchange,[13] there is value in presenting in a schematic way a general process of change since the nineteenth century. In this presentation, the pre-colonial period, pre-1880 approximately, can be characterized by the *dala* residential unit organized largely for its own consumption needs; and by careful organization of household resources to assure the rich harvests that nature would allow, yet with important participation in the exchange circuits of the Lake Victoria region. Cattle, iron goods, salt, pottery, and fish, among other commodities, moved along these circuits.

With the colonial period, new pressures and tensions were, according to this model, introduced: first, to turn production toward the generation of surpluses for colonial and world markets, which would bring, it was thought, rich returns for the economy of the metropolitan country; and, second, to generate cash income to support, through various forms of taxation, the local colonial establishment and additional cash income to stimulate the import market for goods manufactured in the metropolitan country. Through incentives and coercion — new tastes, previously unavailable manufactures, taxes, seizures, colonial production quotas set for local headmen, and forced labour — the production of surpluses for colonial and world markets was stimulated across the entire East African region.

In some locations, the colonial stimulus worked swiftly. In other areas, the colonial programme to expand production became a battlefield of contention. African farmers saw difficulties, uncertainties, and dangers in redirecting their household resources into new forms of production. For them, questions of labour supply, food security (including nutrition and taste), and economic return became immediate ones, and involved the intimate relations among members of the household. Who could the household feed? How should the household reschedule cultivating and planting to optimize the production of world market commodities such as cotton or coffee, on the one hand, and foodstuffs for household consumption and local and colonial markets — maize, peas, beans, sesame, millet, and sorghum — on the other? How does one mix the keeping of livestock with this production? How far could fallow lands be disturbed to extend production? Is it worthwhile to claim and open for production virgin forest? How much additional labour did the household need to aggregate? How does one force up the productivity of family members? How does one store and save foodstuffs and income for hard times? How can the household improve its market position by varying the timing of carrying goods to market and by using different markets and buyers? How far should one follow the extensive advice of colonial agricultural officials? For other household members, these and other questions arose. Who governs the household? Who inherits the authority of the household, its resources, and its production? How does one augment income from outside farm production? Who directs the expenditure of the household income? What are the optimum uses of this income?

These were questions that were not easily resolved, though the household discourse over their resolution was far removed 'from the colonial authorities and commercial officials, who kept pressing for more and more agricultural production for the colonial markets. Often these struggles over the construction or reconstruction of household production were raised into public view in peasant struggles against colonial coercion, colonial regulations, exploitative markets and, later, in the anti-colonial nationalist movements. The issue of the rights of households to shape their own mix of production was carried by farmers into the colonial political arena.

Africans most readily saw colonial agricultural programmes as arrangements for the capture of their wealth and their labour. They also saw these programmes placing African households in jeopardy because of periodic famine. In the Chagga region of Tanzania (then German East Africa), an extraction of male labour from old farms to European farms was observed in the first decade of this century; and it became commonplace through this century to note for almost any area of eastern Africa that only the elderly, women, and young children worked the fields of African farms. In Uganda, Langi farmers resisted for two decades — into the 1920s — considerable pressure from British officials to turn their production from sesame (which they had produced for regional markets for many decades) to cotton for the imperial market.[14]

Some African peasants and peasant leaders sought more lucrative market conditions and were prepared, under certain conditions, to move more fully into production for the market. In Kenya, some African farmers in one section of Machakos District moved vigorously into market gardening of fruits and vegetables, carrying them to urban markets, themselves introducing ox-ploughing to extend production. The new market position these farmers achieved in the 1920s and early 1930s was feared by the European settlers of Kenya, who sought the protection provided by stiff production and marketing regulations to maintain their domination of these markets.[15]

For the Europeans, Kamba competition was quite visible, as they daily saw the heavy traffic of Africans and produce moving between Kamba farms and the peri-urban and urban markets of Nairobi. Paradoxically, while European farmers could be quite troubled by the marketing successes of their African neighbours, the European officers in the district stations of eastern Africa saw the chief problem as one of breaking what they saw as the ancient conservative, subsistence routines of the notional African household. Using taxes here, pressing chiefs and headmen there, the European officers saw themselves guiding Africans, often against their will, from a mentality of subsistence to one of surplus commodity production for the markets.

In time — continuing this schematic history of the path from abundance to poverty — African production over this region of plenty was so transformed through commercialization that the 'balance of nature' was disturbed through overplanting, under-fallowing, decimation of forests, and terrible erosion. The commercialization process had fully exposed African households to the uncertainties of the world markets in cotton, groundnuts, sisal, cloves, sugar, and vegetable oils. The African producers' responses to these uncertainties, like the responses of farmers throughout the world, were, at first, to invest more resources and to expand production to safeguard household incomes, even if households were to be at risk in the long run. At some moments, these household decisions, aggregated a hundred thousand times, generated growth in the colonial economy.

This growth path of colonial agricultural commodity production could not be sustained, given the vagaries of the world markets, the deterioration of the physical environment and the considerable extraction of labour from African farms. The later colonial governments, the newly independent African governments, and members of the households of African producers began to turn to other possible sources of income and to let capital and labour drain from the arena of rural production. What is observed today is a 'food crisis' of continental scale, in which predominantly rural countries are unable to sustain their own food supply, where severe damage has been done to Africa's natural resources, and where hunger, as opposed to abundance, is the first observation of the traveller into rural Africa.

During the colonial era, the reworked authority of the colonial state used various sanctions, including physical force and taxation, to turn the 'production of abundance' toward the supply of commodities for world and colonial markets. However, African producers in some areas came to see these pressures as more

73

benign and less violent than those that had been imposed by the pre-colonial states. Indeed, there was a glow of satisfaction concerning the relief from tribute extractions that colonial governance seemed to promise. Yet other African producers responded with fear and contempt to the physical force and taxation programmes of the colonial state. They were aware of the dangers inherent in the colonial promotion of a shift of production from domestically consumed foodstuffs to cotton and they feared the forms of labour control of large-scale plantation systems introduced in some areas, particularly to promote the sugar crop.

In response, African producers worked out innumerable forms of overt and covert resistance. Tax avoidance and tax revolts were commonplace. Over most of the region, Africans moved into new production at a pace and in ways that were different to what the commanding colonial power sought. Many households withdrew from production for the market as a way of maintaining a separation from the exploitative elements of the colonial economy. Self-sufficiency (and with it a subsistence orientation) did not in the colonial period necessarily imply the 'irrational' retention of ancient, conservative and backward economic practices. Rather, it could be a decisive positive response to the poor terms offered in colonial markets.[16] From the viewpoint of different observers, it could be simultaneously backward agriculture; or fields worked only by women, children, and the elderly; or a means of conservation of scarce resources while members of the household migrated for wage labour.

Significantly, in these arenas of colonial agriculture, hundreds of thousands of individuals saw their future and security not in agriculture but rather in other pursuits. Young African producers were ready to 'make peace' with the colonial state, but not as agricultural producers; rather, they were leaving the land in large numbers to attempt to join an emerging wage-labour force. And when, for whatever reason, they returned to their homes in the countryside, they saw the rural arena and the little village as a promising setting for small business investments in bars, hotels, shops, and houses for rental. These investments have dramatically altered the look of the countryside and have in certain paradoxical ways made the capital cities and the countryside less dissimilar, but not less distinctive in terms of wealth. The old rural and village markets of Kenya, Tanzania, and Uganda fill up with folk twice a week but there are few sales and pockets are almost empty. The little Boro market of western Kenya today could robe a considerable nineteenth-century caravan with the cast-off clothes of the middle classes of European and American cities (cast-off clothing being the most common article in the markets of western Kenya), but the same caravan would starve if it had to live off the food surpluses carried twice weekly to the Boro market.

In Africa, the colonial state was superficially powerful, attempting to take control of virtually every realm of life and extending to the level of household production. But behind the mask of authority there was a critical weakness. The colonial state could not capture the productive efforts of the African household according to plan and its efforts to do so often led — as did the more virulent tribute collections of the pre-colonial state — to the weakening of production. But the colonial state had a much weaker claim on the production and product of the household than did the pre-colonial state. In post-colonial Africa, the newly independent states carried forward the colonial mask of authority. Indeed, much of the apparatus of nationalist movements, of the political culture of the new states of Africa, contributed to the embellishment of this mask without, for the most part, re-establishing the deep claim upon the production and product of the household that had been pervasive in the pre-colonial era. Nationalist leaders drew support from rural Africans by letting them believe that independence meant relief from those intrusive and extractive policies of the colonial state that did actually function.

In the 1960s, at the time of independence of Kenya, Uganda, and Tanzania, there was a feeling abroad that strong demand for tropical products in the world market, technical improvements in the production, marketing, and transport of agricultural products, a better mix of production, and simple patriotic spirit would unleash the riches of labour and physical resources of the region. But, within a few years, observers and participants alike recognized the signs of failure in agriculture throughout the Lake Victoria region. What was perhaps barely recognized at all was the extent to which the generation of plenitude and the image of tropical abundance in the past rested not on nature but on prevalent political conditions. The abundance witnessed by the European traveller and recalled with warmth by the older African today was generated by elaborate forms of state coercion, which more recent struggle has made irreproducible.

Time of the butchers

The epizootics that raged between 1880 and 1900 devastated the herds of western Kenya. People of Siaya remember *Apamo*, the rinderpest epidemic of 1890-2. Each disease episode was followed by a period of intensive rebuilding of stocks, of reconstituting wealth, through exchanges between areas of greater and lesser loss. The exchanges that made possible the rebuilding of herds were constructed from the enduring economic relations between Dholuo-speakers and non-Dholuo-speakers, which had developed across frontier areas in earlier decades. In the southern areas, Jo-Karachuonyo made use of relations with Abagusii groups, and Jo-Kamyamkago groups benefited from associations with the Isiria Maasai. To the north, long-established exchange relations between Dholuo-speakers and non-Dholuo-speakers in the areas of present Sakwa, Gem, Ugenya, and Samia provided opportunities for the replenishing of livestock wealth after these episodes of cattle disease. The confiscations of cattle by early colonial agents, and their delegated authorities, provided a new kind of 'epizootic', continuous with older patterns of cattle-raiding in the sense that stock was *lost*; but new in the sense that reverse and compensatory raiding could not be undertaken to *augment* stock.

In Siaya, oral narratives recall favourable pastures in upper Asembo, around Lake Gangu in Alego, and in Gem Kathomo, before the era of the epizootics. Through the 1880s, 1890s, and early 1900s, exchange relations were sufficiently productive to allow for the reconstitution of herds. And much of the pastures remained fertile and safe for grazing. By 1900, there evidently existed large herds of cattle in Siaya, the Kano plains, and in South Nyanza; the colonial authorities saw cattle as a source of wealth that could pay some of the costs of the colonial establishment in western Kenya and they saw cattle also as a source of a problem. The *japith*, the 'owner of the herd', gained ascendancy over the *janam*, the 'river-lake fisherman', as the endearing persona of Luo songs and poetry of the early part of the century.

One is teased toward a recognition that an economy and a culture organized around the holding and exchange of cattle was a formed and not a given feature[17] of the western Kenya landscape; that the poetics of cattle in Siaya has its specific historical moment and authors. Its context may lie not in an ancient 'cattle complex' conveyed from the southern Sudan but rather in the struggles to rebuild wealth after the epizootics, with their accompanying intense focus on cattle exchanges and management.

The importance of cattle exchanges — the 'cattle trade' — as a means of replenishing herds, as a means of private accumulation, and as a way of alleviating famine, is echoed in the oral narratives that refer to pre-colonial and colonial western Kenya. In the early decades of the twentieth century the 'cattle trade' was simultaneously both a 'centrepiece' of relations between Africans and Europeans and a hidden arena in which herds were concealed from investigators, placed outside the reach of regulations, and moved to official and unofficial markets away from roads, and out of view, without permits. The scale of herds and the scale of traffic cannot be measured with any precision; indeed, the cattle economy presents its own critique of the competency of colonial statistics and the effectiveness of colonial regulation.

The movement and exchange of surplus cattle — and of hides and ghee — offered owners of herds, transporters, and African brokers a ready entry into the monetized economy of twentieth-century western Kenya. From Kisumu, Mumias, Yala, and Karungu came Arab, Swahili, Indian, and European traders and trading companies that pressed their demands forward into the Siaya countryside.[18] From the beginning of the century until the Second World War, these traders collected cattle, ghee, skins, and other products, including sesame and finger millet, from new and budding markets that dotted the countryside.

Matthias Ogutu's forthcoming work on the growth of market centres in Marachi offers a useful model for the depiction of the development of such markets in Siaya. Ogutu has constructed a picture of the simultaneous evolution of markets, exchange rates and market principles and routines, and the actual physical constitution of market centres. The permanent market centre, the regularized market days, the identifiable local traders — both male and female — became routine features of the countryside during this period. Carrying produce, or driving cattle to a particular market, according to a recognized schedule of date and time, and working with a known coterie of market traders and figures, became routine for people across Siaya well before 1939.

But the 'cattle trade' was not a stable and predictable element in Siaya. Periodic droughts, and new roads and settlements, reduced the scale of the pastures. Rinderpest and pleuro-pneumonia reduced the Siaya herds in 1905-6, 1918-19, and 1923, and replenishment of herds became more difficult. As well, market strategies, the sharply increased cost of living after the First World War, and colonial tax and veterinary controls — after the epizootics, the colonial government enforced destocking, quarantines, cattle-branding, and innoculations — further contributed to the reduction of stocks. Siaya became poor in cattle and began, from the 1920s, to import cattle from Nandi, Kericho, South Nyanza, Kakamega, and eastern Uganda. Cattle markets developed along the frontiers of Siaya: Lubao market in Kakamega, Sondu on the Kipsigis border, Nzoia on the Bukhayo border. These specific markets became large entrepôts at which cattle traders purchased livestock for the Siaya markets, an inversion of the pattern of supply of previous decades. These traders moved the cattle to 'interior' markets in Siaya: Boro, Akala, and Ng'iya, where they were killed for meat, sold to butchers from other markets, or purchased as part of continuing efforts to replenish herds in Siaya.

The transformations in the patterns of supply and demand in and around Siaya, and the new epizootics, gave a considerable edge to traders who figured out how to turn over stock quickly, work their way around colonial regulations, and maximize relations across the Siaya borderlands. Those who saw clearly, and early, that Siaya was quickly transforming itself from a producer of cattle to a consumer of meat, emerged as precocious accumulators in the Siaya countryside. Sila Omolo Oluoch in Gem, Omumbo Achola in Kano, Muna Abele in Siaya market, and Asin Fura in Ndere were some of the first to establish themselves in the vanguard of the local trade. Some established themselves in the early markets. Others, for example Asin Fura, created new markets, sometimes locally known after their names: Asin's market (which became Ndere), Ahindi's market (which became Siaya town), Otoro's market (which became Funyula), and Ndonji's market (which became Ugunja).

While these entrepreneurs provided the capital to finance their sections of the trade and to construct permanent establishments for selling cattle and meat, an important element of the 'cattle trade' in Siaya was the youth, who turned themselves into a guild of cattle walkers, the *josemb dhok*. These young men were the real technicians of the trade. They evolved the specific extensive networks of trade routes, worked out patterns of co-operation with the inhabitants of the locations through which they traversed and exchanged information about cattle diseases, police operations, cattle rustlers, and market fluctuations. The 'cattle trade' and its networks were constituted amidst hazards that could not be removed.

Since the 'cattle trade' was a business transacted on the march, friendships and bonds of trust among *josemb dhok* and people along the routes came to be of the utmost importance. Over time, the cattle traders and the *josemb dhok* together — but at two distinct levels of specificity — developed a profound knowledge of the landscape, demography and conditions along the routes from neighbouring lands into and across Siaya. From two informants like Owino Kongo, a cattle trader and butcher of Rang'ala, and his chief *jasemb dhok*, Omondi Oyal, one can learn, in the space of an afternoon, a large amount about the weather, cattle values, police vigilance, anticipated profits and losses, the propensity to bribery of officials in the region, over a wide terrain covering lower Kakamega, Kisumu, South Nyanza, Siaya, and Busia districts. Their testimony is both intimate and general, full of adventure and also of hazard. Some of their knowledge they share with anyone whom they may encounter; other knowledge may be held close to the chest.

The memories of the cattle traders recall a time, in the 1920s and 1930s, when real fortunes were made by those who were willing to hazard the long 'cattle walk' from Siaya to eastern Uganda. There were and are stories of incredible danger, and of failure as well as success. Some fortune-seekers like James Oganga of Liganua were cheated and knifed by their counterparts on the slopes of Mount Elgon in the period 1902-4. Others, like Joseph Wayodi, successfully walked as far as the Akokoro and Dokolo counties of southern Lango in Uganda, there to make a lasting association and friendship with Opeto, Milton Obote's father, and a cattle trader in his own right. Yet others, like Ng'ong'o Ratil, recall long journeys into Bukedea in eastern Uganda in the 1920s, with younger brother Albert Osur in tow to learn the ropes. Eastern Uganda was the preferred long-distance trade route, at least until the intervention of Idi Amin. But other important routes were operated by Siaya traders and walkers: running all the way from northern Tanzania through Karungu and Karachuonyo to Sondu market, and from Maliboi (Eldama Ravine) via Lubao to Ugunja.

The 'cattle trade' has always generated rumours that cattle traders were involved in cattle rustling and thieving on the side. Certainly, known cattle thieves such as Mamba Abur of Kaluo and another gentleman of Nyakach Kabodho have always claimed when caught that they were in the employment of some cattle trader or other. Their claims, their confessions, and the stories told about them, have gone some way to reinforce a perspective of many people in Siaya that the accumulations of capital out of cattle involved not only acumen, but also luck, magic, graft, and thieving. In an important sense, the cattle trade was so complex, the routines of exchange so closed to public view, the methods of accounting profit and loss so obscure, that it is understandable that people outside the trade would not fully comprehend that profit and accumulation could come from carefully organized buying and selling of livestock.

Fortunes were quickly made, yet they were also sometimes quickly lost through risks such as holding cattle during an outbreak of disease, or losses due to rustling. The cattle traders knew, and the *josemb dhok* understood, that success in the trade rested in part on disposing of their 'merchandise' as soon as possible. This was an incentive to the *josemb dhok* to speed up their activities and to accumulate new information about markets and routes that would allow an acceleration of transport.

There was also an incentive to move into, or enlarge the scale of, butchering of cattle. Some of the most successful early traders: Sila Omolo, Muna Abele, and Asin Fura, doubled as butchers, and became pioneer figures in the establishment of permanent markets and rural towns around their butcheries, a process evident in the 1920s and 1930s. One is led to suspect that there were considerable and important changes in the patterns of culling food ('shopping') and in diet in Siaya in this period, these changes turning on the cash purchase of small cuts of meat from the butcheries. In one sense, the opening of this pattern of purchase closed the circle of transformation from a cattle exporting to a meat consuming region. On the other it is an early example of the 'break-bulk' purchase and consumption pattern in the cash economy, where new profits were to be won from the resale of commodities in smaller quantities to the Siaya population. Further, one might observe that under the changing conditions of the 1920s and 1930s what had been the foremost store of wealth or capital — cattle — was now being cut up, sold, and served as food.

A further observation is that the 'break-bulk' profit from the butcheries — a new form of accumulation — was reinvested in diverse and specific ways. Sila Omolo Oluoch and Asin Fura invested in permanent shops and butcheries. Omumbo Achola invested in large shops and taxi services in Kisumu town. Owino Kongo invested in semi-permanent houses in his rural Liganua home. All of them used their new capital to 'acquire' more wives. None used their capital for the extended education of their children.

The 'cattle trade' and the development of butcheries in Siaya were at the core of 'rural urbanization', both visibly and in terms of the structures of wealth accumulation and the distribution of economic activities in the countryside. The butchery evolved as a specialized activity and became enduring property of new lineages. The several individual decisions of butchers to transfer proprietorship and skills to their sons — rather than sending them to schools to train for other work — has produced continuities in accumulation not available elsewhere, or to others, in the countryside. The Asin Fura family of Ndere reorganized itself around the butchery founded there in 1924. The butchery expanded into a shop, in the 1950s a tea room was added, and then, in the 1970s, the family extended its activities into motor transport.

It would, however, be a mistake to assume that accumulation in the Asin Fura family translated directly into the concentration of wealth. Asin Fura had a pack of sons, and much of the accumulation from the butchery and from the newer and associated activities has gone into the payment of bridewealth and the construction of homesteads for the sons in and near Ndere. As a consequence of this pattern of accumulation and expenditure, no member of the Asin Fura family went elsewhere seeking work or opportunities. The sons never worked in wage employment. New capital has been effectively deconstituted as capital.

Today, the sons are puzzled by the idioms of the modern capitalist economy: the licences, deeds, inspectors, latrine regulations . . . all these are seen as unnecessary and painful intrusions of a bothersome state. There are other concerns about state intervention. In years past, some complaints were centred on the haphazard nature of the state's intervention: that a cattle market would be closed on scant rumour of an illness in an area, and that the orders would continue week after week without any specific check of the information. Butchers interviewed at Siaya, Ndere, and Otonglo markets in mid-1986 expressed the opinion that the state had arbitrarily intervened to set meat prices at a level that was way out of reach of most rural households. 'Nobody is able to afford twenty-five shillings for a kilo of meat.' So instead of slaughtering two or three cattle a day at Rangala, as was the case in the mid-1970s, Owingo Kongo now has to be content with two a week, not to mention the wastage from having no refrigeration for his unsold meat. The sons of the accumulators of the 1920s are now being consumed by the conditions of a market that they cannot influence or remake.

Clearly, the history of the cattle trade and the butcheries in Siaya is also one edge of the history of the *state* in Kenya and the relation of the state to production, exchange, and consumption. The *josemb dhok* and *jopith* define the reach of the state as they sequester or rush their cattle through the Siaya countryside. And while they recognized the agents and laws of the colonial state as a competitive and invasive apparatus, they, with the butchers, moved their capital into new ventures made possible by state reorganization of the regional economy. The evolution of the Siaya butcheries, as with the emergence of a maize culture in Siaya, became a temporal context in which the state in Kenya was recognized, comprehended, and represented in the thought and expression of people of Siaya as a sometimes irrational and often invasive and competing organism.

Social scientists examining late colonial and post-colonial Kenya have focused attention on the workplace — factories, docks, railways and large farms and estates — and the city as the crucibles for the formation of new political consciousness and new politically radical and progressive associations. There is a nagging sense in the general approach that suggests Kenyans must enter directly and physically into the sector of European-formed capitalism to achieve a comprehension of the framework of domination that defines the world of the individual. In time, according to this interpretation, the newly evolving consciousness seeps back to the countryside, to the backward labour reserves of western Kenya, through the general circulation of information and through the return of workers to their home areas. If responses to oppressive conditions are to emerge, according to this view, they will develop in urban areas around labour unrest, unemployment, housing and food shortages, and in response to unrestrained police violence against crowds, students, and workers. Rural areas will remain politically and ideologically backward until cadres of the new Kenya reach out to, and educate, their countryfolk. Events and experience in Siaya suggest that an interpretation that segments Kenya into crucibles and backwaters of this sort is inaccurate. The work of comprehending an elaborate and complex process of domination is and has been going on in rural Siaya in a way that is relatively integrated with and simultaneous with the experience of Siaya folk in the cities.

In this regard the material from Siaya presents itself in two different voices. The people of Liganua stand immobilized around the prone Obalo as if waiting for the intervention of a more substantial science, while the sons of the butchers profess an incapacity to deal with the complexities of state intervention in the market economy. Yet in the behaviour of the *josemb dhok* and the *jopith* and in the discourses on maize and the *gorogoro* economy, folk of Siaya, denizens of a backwater labour reserve distant from Nairobi, claim a comprehension of the language of political domination in Kenya, while those in authority seem to be a long way off grasping an understanding of the array of intelligence and sensitivity that is present in the labour reserve. Political consciousness may be raised in the great crucibles of the cities and workplace, but it is also raised simultaneously amidst what is disparagingly referred to as the 'idiocy of rural life'.

NOTES

1. Remark occasionally heard in Siaya conversation.
2. Oginga Odinga, *Not Yet Uhuru: An Autobiography* (New York, Hill and Wang, 1969), p. 7.
3. Ralph Herring, 'The influence of climate on the migrations of the central

and southern Lwo', *Kenya Historical Review*, 4, 1 (1976), p. 39. See Margaret Jean Hay, 'Economic Change in Luoland: Kowe, 1890-1945', PhD dissertation, University of Wisconsin, Madison, 1972, pp. 94-7; this provides a brief discussion of the production of sorghum in Kowe, in western Kenya. For a treatment of the larger colonial economy, see Hugh Fearn, *An African Economy: A Study of the Economic Development of Nyanza Province of Kenya, 1903-1953* (London, Oxford University Press, 1956).

4. By the beginning of the twentieth century vocabulary drew a distinction that explicitly referred to the difference between maize and the old staples; a distinction between 'food' (*chiemo* in Dholuo) and 'ration' (*posho*). See David William Cohen, 'Food production and food exchange in the precolonial Lakes Plateau region', in Robert I. Rotberg (ed.), *Imperialism, Colonialism, and Hunger: East and Central Africa* (Lexington, Mass., Lexington Books, 1983), p. 14.

5. For maize in western Kenya, see Hay, 'Economic change in Luoland', Chapters 5-7, and, for South Nyanza, see Judith Mariann Butterman, 'Luo social formations in change: Karachuonyo and Kanyamkago, c. 1800-1945', PhD dissertation, Syracuse University, 1979, Chapter 5. Dale L. Hutchnison and Clark Spence Larsen have studied a sixteenth-century episode of a newly established maize diet in the Spanish—Indian contact setting of St Catherine's Island in the American South through the chemical analysis of skeletal remains. They note raised levels of physiological stress, growth disruption and fall in life expectancy from the pre-maize agricultural era. 'The increase in emphasis on maize agriculture as revealed by the analysis of bone chemistry most likely reflects the increase in demand placed on native populations for feeding not only themselves but the Europeans in the region as well.' 'Stress and adaptation at Santa Catalina de Guale: analysis of human remains', paper presented at the Society for Historical Archaeology, 9 January 1987, p. 7.

6. This is a joke frequently told from the 1950s up to the present. It suggests the hopelessness in the economic position of the segmented household, combining wage labour in the urban area and small-plot farming in the western Kenya countryside. Cassava is planted as a precaution against financial failure and hunger.

7. Meja Mwangi, *Going Down River Road* (London, Heinemann, 1976), p. 164.

8. This discussion of the regional food economy is drawn from David William Cohen, 'Natur und Kampf — Uberfluss und Armut in der Viktoriasee-Region in Afrika von 1880 bis zur Gegenwart', *SOWI*, 14, 1 (1985), pp. 10-23. Also, Cohen, 'Food production'.

9. See Margaret Jean Hay, 'Economic Change in late nineteenth century Kowe, Western Kenya', in B. A. Ogot (ed.), *Economic and Social History of East Africa* (Nairobi, East African Literature Bureau, 1975), pp. 90-107.

10. See Margaret Jean Hay, 'Local trade and ethnicity in western Kenya, *African Economic History Review*, 2, 1 (1975), pp. 7-12, and also Hay, 'Economic change in late nineteenth-century Kowe', Lawrence D. Schiller, 'Gem and Kano: a comparative study of stress in two traditional African political systems in Nyanza Province, western Kenya, c. 1850-1914', University of Nairobi History Seminar Paper, 1977; and the unpublished work of Ralph Herring, 'The JoLuo before 1900', paper presented to University of Nairobi History Seminar, March, 1978; and Priscilla O. Were, 'The origin and growth of the iron industry and trade in Samia (Kenya)', BA dissertation, University of Nairobi, 1972.

11. Hay, 'Economic change in late nineteenth-century Kowe', pp. 100-1.

12. Herring, 'The JoLuo'.

13. The characterization of 'subsistence' holds that the domain of food was largely local, enclosed, stable, and autonomous from the political sphere before the entry of colonial forces. Given what we do know about the exchange of surpluses and regional trade circuits in the nineteenth century (see Cohen, 'Food production'), there are problems with the unmediated application of a concept of subsistence to these production units.

14. John Tosh, 'Lango agriculture during the early colonial period: land and labour in a cash-crop economy', *Journal of African History*, 19, 3 (1978), pp. 415-39.

15. See J. Forbes Munro, *Colonial Rule and the Kamba: Social Change in the Kenya Highlands, 1889-1939* (Oxford, Clarendon Press, 1975).

16. Gerd Spittler, 'Administration in a peasant state', *Sociologia Ruralis*, 23 (1980), pp. 130-44

17. For a rich and discursive treatment of cattle exchange, rituals involving cattle, cattle as bridewealth, and cattle as meat, see A. B. C. Ocholla-Ayayo, 'Marriage and cattle exchange among the Nilotic Luo', *Paideuma*, 25 (1979), pp. 173-93.

18. See, in particular, Butterman, 'Luo social formations'; and Hay, 'Economic change in Luoland'.

The Powers of   V
Women

Luo men talk about women as a social category, and there are
many conversations about women generally. On the road from
Agulu to Ndere, on market day, men of different ages stroll down
the road discussing women and presenting remarkably ambi-
valent and variable conclusions on the place and power of
women. One of them may suggest that 'proper women are
women who know how to subordinate themselves to men', and
that 'this is the way it should be'. Another may remark that 'this
is hardly the way women behave', for there are uncountable
examples of women assuming major roles, of seizing the initiative
from the men — fathers, brothers, husbands, and sons —
around them. Still another may remark that certain women 'have
the power to tame men'; 'they wield powerful words and have
learned the secrets of imposing their will upon their husbands'.
Some men may at one moment disparage the idea of women
as powerful, yet at another moment express pride in a particular
woman's achievements.

It is not a question which is easy for men of Siaya to settle;
and it is no easier for all the voices that refer to the station of
women in the wider society. There are sayings, often repeated,
for example:

'Odhako Rachieno', 'Woman, wearer of the traditional Chieno'.
('The woman can dare you.')
'Dhako halabotene ok hep.' 'A man cannot successfully duck
the darts of a woman.'

There is also a song that men sing in the bars:

> *Solo*: Kir unyiedh mon
> *Chorus*: Mon Kinyiedhi
> *Solo*: Yamo biro marang'ongo
> Ogot won Opiche
> Be unyiedho mon

> *Chorus*: Mon Kinyiedhi
> Yamo Ohingo mon.
> Dare you tether women?
> You dare not/There's no way.
> There is an epidemic abroad.
> Ogot, son of Opiche
> Dare you milk women?
> You dare not.
> They are hooked into the epidemic.

Stories are commonly told of the interventions of powerful potions and magic into the relations between women and men. It was reported in Mombasa in 1978 that A., a young Alego girl married to R., a Gem man, had given her husband a love potion. This was a piece of crocodile meat that she had boiled in his supper. R. became ill and it was feared he would die. A. panicked and confessed her deed to R.'s uncle, M. She had been advised of the love potion by an Akamba woman friend and a fellow primary school teacher.

There is another song which celebrates a woman for having built a homestead for herself.

> Meru Ogoyo dala
> Meru gangla
> Olang'o K'Obilo
> Min Ogoyo dala
> Meru gangla
> Kara meru Thuon
>
> Your mother built a home!
> She's extraordinary
> Olang'o K'Obilo
> Your mother built a home!
> She's wonderful
> She's a warrior!

The migrations of male labour have provided opportunities for this sort of initiative on the part of women and, in years to come, they may become routine. Because the men — husbands, fathers, brothers, and sons — are away from home for so long, the women have in fact become heads of rural households.

The pressure to adjust to a marriage falls primarily on the woman. Women say they must please their husbands, avoid complaining too much, and not be 'too stubborn'. This is not to suggest that women conform automatically to their husband's wishes. Luo women have their rights and show considerable strength in caring for themselves and their children.

Personalities also vary, as some women tend to be dominant, others are quarrelsome, and still others use persuasion or subterfuge to get what they want. However, a woman is constrained to comply outwardly with her husband's wishes and to avoid openly opposing him to the point of unresolvable conflict. Women have few formal means of altering the domestic situation. In a real sense they do not have the option of terminating their marriage and therefore cannot issue any ultimate threat. Thus, women say they can do little to affect the man's behaviour. In cases of a 'good' marriage, it may be possible to talk to the husband. If he refuses to co-operate, there is not much the wife can do.[1]

Some see these stories of women taking initiatives in the countryside, assuming authority from their male kin or husbands, as a defiance of male authority, or a remaking of gender relations. It is also, clearly, addressed to the extreme hardships involved in surviving in the countryside in the absence of labour and, sometimes for long periods, wages remitted from distant kin. In a sense, as women enlarge their roles, they are showing how material demands may overcome culture.[2]

It is worth considering that this growing reality of women taking over responsibilities in the specific contexts of lineage estates in the countryside grows simultaneously with their migrant kin and husbands being pressured in innumerable ways to invest substantial capital in the renovation or enhancement of the *simba*.

The funeral is a focal issue in Kenya Luo consocation. The vast majority of voluntary, mainly polysegmentary associations in the towns function most effectively as funeral associations. The turnout for a meeting is itself instructive. A typical clan meeting, characteristically called to discuss the issue of *harambee* for a primary school building (for example, of the Umira lineage) will, 'to save money', cloister itself in a two-and-a-half metre by three metre room in Gorofani estate, Nairobi, and conduct its business for a full three or four hours. Perhaps ten or twelve people will attend. But comes a funeral and a licence becomes affordable, and the entire Umira family will turn up at the house of the bereaved on one or more of the seven or eight days when the inevitable collection of funds for funeral expenses takes place. Such funeral gatherings, whether to honour the high or the low, are pivotal in drawing people together.

Luo in the countryside and in the city commonly remark on the sudden, accidental deaths of Luo men, frequently in road accidents. It is commonly supposed among Kenyans that Luo suffer disproportionately from such tragedies; not that they are bad drivers, or that fate runs against the Luo male, but rather because of greater driving distances.

There is an immense and growing pantheon of Luo killed tragically in their own vehicles or in passenger trucks. This high rate of road deaths has produced a new Luo social category: the household of the young widow and young children. Increasingly, the older practice of a wife's being inherited by the victim's male relations — with a return to the country lands — is not recognized and these 'road-widow' families more often remain in Nairobi and organize anew their household economies.

. . .the emotional and economic pull of her children tends to draw a woman back to her original husband's home. . .Inheritance rules also set limits on a woman's options. Since a woman has no rights to land except through marriage, her ability to terminate a marriage is restricted. Without land a woman cannot support herself and has nowhere to go. Either her parents must consent to the separation and permit her return, or she must find a second husband. In this context Luo attitudes towards divorce take on particular importance. A divorced woman's reputation is always suspect. Moreover if she has had children, it is expected that she will eventually return to her first husband's home. Thus her ability to contract a satisfactory second marriage is limited. Recognizing this situation, her parents are usually reluctant to consent to her divorce or to accept her back.[3]

There is also evidence that these households eschew the kinds of symbolic investments in the countryside that are characteristic of other households and of men living temporarily in the city. With the deaths of their husbands and the weakening of connections with the husbands' kin, they are released from many of the pressures affecting others in the city. The Luo widows, with accumulated funds, are likely to make economic investments in the city or perhaps in the sugar belt; pressing on with their own careers. Widows like Pamela Mboya, Joanna Argwings-Kodhek, and Mrs Okuthe have established independent domains in the city and have asserted themselves boldly in the national society. While there is patterned rhetoric expressing great concern for a growing army of Luo road widows, the women themselves, apart from the expressions of concern, are making heroic strides to resolve the anomaly and apparent fragility of a female-headed Luo household in present-day Kenya.[4]

There is an important paradox involved in Luo folk worrying about women heading households in the city while simultaneously women assume greater authority in numerous households in the countryside.

An economy of therapy

Siaya District Hospital, located in the town of Siaya, and part of a network of nationally regulated hospitals, was founded in 1972. At a number of sites in Siaya there are dispensaries and clinics with staff recognized by the national medical service. Often, alongside these clinics, or interspersed among them, are a number of *dukas* (stores), where medicines, and medical advice, from various sources can be acquired. There is, additionally, a range of specialists respected in the use of herbs and other treatments. All through the countryside are the stations of *daktari* — often former medical assistants — whose stations are organized into clinics and wards. There are also the itinerant *daktaris* on their bicycles, travelling the countryside and equipped and ready to give injections. And there are the compounds and homesteads of gifted women who offer long-term therapy and hospitalization for specific, yet not otherwise treatable, illnesses.

There is in Siaya a well-defined therapeutic economy. Considerable expenditure is devoted to health care away from the national health stations. And within therapy there is a distinctive landscape. Women like Isabella of Asego, Marcella of Liganua, and Maria of Boro, who offer the long-term services in their homes or specially organized compounds, may treat upwards of several hundred people simultaneously. Collecting funds, livestock, and labour as payment for their services, these women have become considerable accumulators. There are costs, however, beyond the expenses of maintaining a therapeutic household and its many denizens. Medicine in Siaya can be extremely dangerous. Those who handle medicines routinely may be made ill by their power. Stories are common of therapeutic practitioners who have died horrible deaths as a consequence of handling all-too-powerful medications.

The economy of therapy is also about traffic: the movement of the ill, concerned friends and kin, and the practitioners around the countryside and around Kenya in search of, respectively, effective treatment and more opportunities for practice. The taxi, the car, the bus, are significant elements of the long-distance economy of therapy as patients move back and forth along the highways seeking the best in specialized care. The traffic also marks the economy of therapy as substantially experimental, and this is how most Luo in western Kenya view the landscape of therapy; as an experimental terrain across which one must travel to seek improved diagnosis and effective treatment.

One significant element of the therapeutic economy is that the people of Siaya seem generally to value the medications and therapies that they pay for in the countryside more highly than the medications and treatments offered free at the Siaya District Hospital and health service dispensaries and clinics. It is commonplace for individuals travelling to Siaya Hospital for treatment to stop at market centres along the way and pay for the services of a *daktari*. Many explanations are given for the priorities attached to therapies offered outside the national medical services. For one, Siaya District Hospital staff members, most often rotated in from other areas, are not known to the people of Siaya,   *89* who express openly the need to know an inside person at the hospital to assure adequate and efficacious treatment. It is a widely held opinion of prospective patients that Siaya District Hospital doctors prescribe aspirin for every ailment or, alternatively, that they never give adequate dosages because the drugs are provided free. Many express the view that 'injections are the only real medication that the Siaya Hospitals should offer' and people feel ill-treated if injections are not given. By contrast, the *daktari* gives injections more routinely.[5]

One story from Boro illustrates part of this therapeutic economy. Onam was a cook, a strong 15-year-old from a poor home a few kilometres from Boro. Onam had never had an affair with a girl and this fact was a subject of much ribbing among the collection of young men and women who hovered around the archaeological camp. Venereal disease has been a subject of continuous concern to the young in Kenya. The prevalence of venereal disease has made penicillin a high-value commodity, often sold on the black market, and the scarcity and price of the wonder drug have made the visitor to Kenya the target of inquiry and pleading, since the foreigner is known to carry essential medical supplies wherever he or she goes.

Now during a discussion over tea at the Boro archaeological camp, an argument developed over whether such and such a young woman in Boro had, and was spreading, venereal disease. Onam was adamant that this woman did not, could not, have it; the argument concluded when Onam declared that he was going to prove that this woman was not spreading VD and that he was going to have his first affair in the course of bringing such proof to his friends. A couple of weeks later Onam announced that the deed was done, he was no longer the boy looking for his first affair.

Later, symptoms developed, and these had a varied interpretation in Onam's circle. Onam's friends said, 'Well, Onam, now you have it, VD, and you'd better go to Siaya and get some antibiotics.' Onam responded, 'No, not at all, this is simply what happens when you have intercourse the first time.' Onam got worse and finally went to the local dispensary and told them, by his own recollection, that he was suffering from a case of 'first intercourse', basically, as 'Dr' Onam saw it, a terrible irritation. The medical assistant in Boro gave Onam some salve to apply and sent him away. Onam then announced that if he had further intercourse, he would no longer be suffering from the 'first intercourse' syndrome. He used the salve, but went off to effect a cure by his own prescribed method.

Within a week or so, the word had spread, and no woman

in the Boro area would go near Onam. Now everybody in Onam's circle — it was becoming a veritable orbit — was telling him that he had better go to Siaya hospital and get the penicillin. Onam resisted. He went back to the Boro medical assistant and asked for a different salve. The medical assistant told Onam to go to Siaya Hospital. Onam said he would not go, he would treat himself. One person in the camp eventually got a chance to talk to Onam privately — and such privacy was very rare in the archaeological camp — and asked him why he would not go to Siaya Hospital, believing he was suffering from an overarching pride as well as VD. Onam said, 'Look, to go to Siaya costs me three shillings, to return costs me three shillings. I will have to go many times before they give me the penicillin. They may not have any to give. They may tell me I have to buy it from so and so. I will only be able to buy a little at a time. I will have to go back again and again. I will be poor again before I finish the treatment.'

Eventually Onam got the attention he required but it was a stunning analysis that he offered. Economic calculation, and the fear of a poor young man being driven back into poverty and greater dependence and forced down from the bottom rung of a ladder of mobility in the Kenya of 1979 and 1980, had generated a response to medical advice and practice that might be misconstrued as a personal struggle between modern and traditional medical practice, or as an example of incomplete reception of scientific information. But the young Onam was no ignorant bumpkin, or silly fool; rather, his analysis and action was anchored in a precocious understanding of the social and economic architecture of contemporary Kenya.

Ochola found himself in a part of the forest where he had never been before. He felt feverish and the blood drummed in his ears. His eyes were swollen and painful from the glare of the bright sunlight. His body was sore. The hairs on his skin stood up in thorn-like warts, pricking his body till he became listless with pain. He could not sit down or lie on his side. When the wind blew hard, he felt as if his whole flesh was being torn away.[6]

There is also a landscape within therapy. It is commonly held that medicines and therapies of other peoples are more powerful than those most immediately available, though this equation does not typically extend to those provided by the national health service, which have long proved themselves, in many Luo minds, to be entirely inadequate. A lovely description of this is to be found in Grace Ogot's novel, *The Promised Land*, where her protagonist, afflicted with a terrible ailment, crosses ethnic boundaries to seek effective therapy. Within Siaya some areas are known to have more powerful medicines and therapies, for example Asembo on the shores of Lake Victoria. Luo may also travel north into Luyia areas in search of more powerful therapies and as far as Kitui in Eastern Province. And some practitioners from Siaya, in particular women, travel seasonally to Nairobi to treat urban Luo and other groups settled in the same quarters of Nairobi, and this practice has proven to be extremely lucrative. The therapeutic economy of western Kenya has located a number of women as substantial accumulators of wealth through the skilful practice of medicine and finance.

Pim's work

In Kenya today, many women and men have occasion to recall the *pim* (old woman) with great affection. The *pim*, in a period of transition from marriage to infirmity, may have come from a considerable social and geographical distance to enter a particular Luo household. She lived with and nurtured the young girls and boys of the household, compound or enclosure, and sometimes the neighbourhood. Boys stayed with the *pim* for several years, leaving her charge when it was seen that they were too old to sleep among the young girls. Girls stayed much longer, often going from the *pim*'s care directly into marriage. And in her new residence, the *pim* herself found shelter, food, support, companionship, and protection.

The *pim* and her charges lived together in the *siwindhe* (the nursery) located within the enclosure or compound. The *siwindhe* consisted of a cohort of children who had reached an age when they should no longer sleep with their parents. Some enclosures had the resources and a budding young population of sufficient size to sustain a *siwindhe* for a long period. But in many settings a few children from here and there would be passed to the care of a *pim* in a nearby enclosure. The *siwindhe* dematerialized as the population of the compound aged, or disappeared.

At about nine o'clock, after hearing the elders, we went to bed, leaving the elders talking among themselves. Young boys and girls slept together in their grandmothers' houses [*siwindhe*], and we were told stories of the past. The older boys went to sleep in the *simba*, a dormitory built near the gates by the grown-up boys who were yet unmarried. Boys grown too big to live in the houses of the old women stayed in the dormitory house and there became acquainted with girls from other villages, and had dances at night.[7]

The *siwindhe* was a building, usually indistinguishable from other domiciles in the compound, at least from the outside. The interior of the *siwindhe* is recalled by those who experienced it as a structure of transition from infancy to maturity. It was within the *siwindhe* that much of the critical social intelligence of the Luo world was imparted by the *pim* to those with little experience or knowledge of it. Children learned about the past from the *pim*. They drew upon her wisdom. They learned about the people, the groups, and the settlements around them. They learned a geography of succour and a geography of danger. They learned about sexuality, about marriage, and about childbirth. And from her wide-ranging social knowledge the *pim* was able to supply information that both broadened and delimited the fields of possible and optimal marriages of her charges. From the *pim*, children learned about magic and the other powers of the world. They learned about health, illness, misfortune, and death. They learned about interest, opportunity, and obligation, factors that would both open up and restrict their lives. As the *pim* nurtured and instructed her charges, linking them with the adult world, the experience she brought from outside the enclosure neighbourhood and from outside the patri-group provided the young with information extending far beyond the patrilineage, and gave them the elements of an intimate understanding of a complex and physically remote social universe.

The *pim* instructed the girls concerning their sexuality. *Pim* taught the girls to be tolerant of their future spouses and in-laws during domestic problems. She taught them about responsibilities of the adult woman and she taught them about the respect due husbands in marriage. *Pim* instructed the girls to refrain from sexual relations outside marriage. A successful union was perceived as being marked from the beginning when a young woman was found to be a virgin, *'en kod ringre'*. The girls were taught never to eat at a boyfriend's house. Secret visitations, *wuowo*, with boyfriends were undertaken at night and girls were instructed to be back before dawn. Such visitations were only known to *pim* and the girls of the *siwindhe*, not to their parents. They were instructed not to visit their boyfriends during menstruation, *dhi boke*. *Pim* taught the girls to offer persistent boyfriends an experience of lovemaking, but without penetration, through the skilful use of the thighs while making love.[8]

In part, the *pim* learned her critical role within the *siwindhe* of her own childhood. In taking up the care of her first charges, she became part of a chain of nurturing extending far into the past. But the *pim* also called upon all her particular experiences of life beyond the *siwindhe*: in marrying, in gathering valuable domestic materials and wild foodstuffs and condiments from the field margins and scrubland, in organizing her cultivation of foods, in cooking and serving, in dealing with illness, in producing and marketing ceramic and fibre wares, in handling childbirth and the care of young children, in living among and learning from women at her husband's home, in moving about to visit and care for friends and relations, in meeting dangerous conditions and forces, in identifying and securing refuges in times of war, famine, and epidemic, in caring for the ancestors, and in discovering pleasures and interests.

In finding a role as a *pim*, the elderly Luo woman also protected herself from a 'social death'; meaning being left to starve amidst   *93* a famine or being otherwise without companionship and protection.[9] Paradoxically, it was this sometimes helpless and dependent figure whose knowledge and experience pierced the fences of the enclosure and the walls of the *siwindhe* and transformed the social intelligence of the young, broadening it to include knowledge of the more extended field of marriage and adulthood, and toward the contingencies, associations, alliances, coalitions, dangers, and opportunities lying beyond the enclosure.

Most marriages were with Luo women from subtribes other than one's own. . .[these were] desirable for strategic reasons. . .if a subtribe were shattered in war, one could go live with affines.[10]

The circulation of social knowledge through the *pim* and within the *siwindhe* extended the horizons of young Luo-speakers and made possible the use of this knowledge, whether in an area twenty kilometres away or over much greater distances in Kampala, Nairobi, and Mombasa. One of the better known of the last *pim* was Granny Muzungu, who was considered to be very knowledgeable about European ways and about Nairobi's society, thus the name 'Muzungu'.[11]

'Granny' Muzungu transformed a distant setting into intimate knowledge. The rich materials of history, of past contacts, of alliances, of old marriages, coalitions, and descent that the *pim* imparted to members of a household later facilitated travel for trade and for social visits. The *pim*'s knowledge contributed to the social expertise carried along on fishing expeditions and marketing enterprises on Lake Victoria. And, likewise, the learning in the *siwindhe* produced invaluable information made use of in individual and household migrations, and in the settlement of new areas. The *pim* deepened the social and geographical knowledge of younger Luo. The new activities, relationships, marriages and mobility that the *pim*'s teachings aided, continuously enlarged the horizons of people across western Kenya.

When we see the importance of social knowledge in the construction of middle-distance and long-distance relations in western Kenya, we are able to understand the pivotal role of childhood socialization in the generation of a regional consciousness and corporateness. Assembled, this knowledge, and the social activity that it animated, gave form to the broader *oganda* associations and was part of the base upon which an active Luo identity — in the form of a 'nation', different from clan or neighbourhood identities — developed.

Before 1930, there may have been thousands of *siwindhe* in western Kenya. But after 1930 there were few. Kisumu, Nairobi, and Mombasa, along with both rural and town schools, promised greater opportunities for the nurturing of the young, while the changing shape of the rural household economy made more problematic the feeding of an elderly and dependent woman coming from outside the home. When, in the late 1960s and early 1970s Ben Blount, a sociolinguist, did research on the acquisition of language of Luo children in western Kenya, he found that a 'young girl ... of 5 or 6 may become the principal caretaker for a younger sibling, assuming the responsibility for feeding the child, protecting him from harm and danger, and catering in general to his needs.'[12] Without access to the memory of the *pim*, and to the material on the evident transformation of childhood socialization in this century, Blount concluded that this absence of adult supervision of children is a 'characteristic of the Luo and closely related Nilotic groups'. One is reminded of how easy it is to accept elements of the present and observed social world as given and traditional.

The *pim*'s nurturing was the crucible of Luo culture and society in the past, yet its critical role has been missed, as anthropologists and historians have attended to the form and play of 'larger', and, in a sense, 'masculine' structures and segmentary processes in Luo society.[13] Until recently, the historical process of development of Luo society in western Kenya has been seen as a process of repetitive, methodical budding, branching and expansion of segments of patrilineal units, a steady segmentation process from a narrow base.

The remaking of Owuodha

Owuodha nyar Odeny, better known as Nyakota after her clan, Kanyakota in Gem, is more than seventy years old. The way she presents herself recapitulates many of the changes taking place in Siaya in the twentieth century. In her youth she was a cultural purist, according to those who remember her, totally opposed to Christianity, particularly to the education of girls and what were referred to as the *timbe jonanga*, 'ways of the clothed "foreignizers"'. She is said to have spoken of the girls who went to school as *okethore* ('deviants'). Nyakota composed a song about them that was sung widely in Alego, Gem, and Ugenya in the 1930s and 1940s:

> Nyar somo timore nadi?
> Dhokchind gweno oluongo no tigo
> Nyar somo ringo gi orenge.

> The educated girl
> See how she behaves

> She consumes chicken
> Calling the intestines 'beads'
> See how she dashes off
> With the chicken's legs!

Having married Odipo Mbai in the late 1930s, Owuodha is one of those who lived on the fringes of the Anglican and Catholic Liganua society for close to thirty years. She was perceived as a virtual non-person, ill-dressed, un-Christian, materially poor . . . until the Legio Maria religion burst forth in 1964. Then Nyakota Owuodha took on a new life. She became a believer and, from the proceeds of the sale of a goat that was part of her daughter's dowry, bought herself a white dress and a rosary, got baptised as Drusila, and became the guardian of the new Legio Maria Church at Liganua. Her Church is one of the many features that have been added to the Siaya landscape by hitherto invisible members of Siaya communities, persons who have donated land and energy to the growth of the Church. Owuodha-Drusila and her Church are the almost imperceptible indications of transformation of the countryside.

'Children of children'

Ligation, known in Dholuo as *tudo*, has been widely reported among unmarried youth. It is a strategy that girls use to protect themselves against premarital sex. One day in 1957, in Ugenya, Mruka Jalam was beating a girl, who was wailing loudly for help, in his *simba*. When the owner of the *dala* intervened, Mruka shouted back that she had 'tied' (bewitched) him, and that she had refused to co-operate in removing the spell. Peace was not restored until Mruka had found the cause under his pillow: three ears of still-green star grass. Mruka later married the girl.

The behaviour of Mruka's friend of the night is in sharp contrast to the image, continually reproduced in the 1930s and 1940s, of the sexually careless, and carefree, schoolgirl, referred to as *amuom nyar skul*, 'the schoolgirl in a hurry'. In contrast to the image of the well-brought-up and chaste brides, there was the figure of the untutored schoolgirl, easily becoming pregnant during the school vacations. These images were, and are, commonly referred to in discourses among young and old in Siaya. These convey instructions to the young and confirm the values of the old. One might also observe that the older people of Siaya find these discourses on sexuality a ready way to affirm the superiority of more general values held, and perceived to be threatened, by the onslaught of *timbe jonanga* (Westernization). The warm memories of the *pim* and the *siwindhe* are part of these discourses on sexuality.

The Siaya countryside, in the 1980s, is striking for the considerable number of 14- and 15-year-olds who are already unwed mothers. One can get a clear view of them at funerals. They are among the gathering holding their babies, a somewhat uncharacteristic image, given that their own mothers are normally nurturing these uninvited grandchildren; at funerals these mothers-cum-grandmothers are too busy caring for guests to hold the infants.

Kwashiorkor-ridden infants are a too eloquent affirmation of the concept of *amuom nyar skul*, of children begetting children before any training in sexual matters has come their way from the adults of the *dala*. The 'children of children' direct our attention to questions of space and distance, for the fathers of many of these infants are themselves teenagers without a *simba* of their own. 'Sex in the grass' — one way it is known in Siaya — also raises questions concerning the intimacy between close cousins, concerns about which are suppressed by adults who fear to expose the identities of fathers of infants produced out of transitory unions between individuals who are too closely related, if not also too young, to marry. Ambrose Adeya Adongo informs us that incest is an ever-present possibility, and fear, in Siaya, but that it is not, cannot be verbalized, though it might be hummed around a beer pot by some elders:

> Osero nyar kewo
> Weuru silwal
> Otum tum pala.

> He woos his cousin!
> Let the light-skinned one
> Wear red ochre [have 'sex in the grass']

The question is also raised as to the sexual mores obtaining in the 'society of the grass'. It is recognized in Kano Kochogo that lax young women do really exist in society. They are nicknamed *gwoma*, 'those who squat willingly'. It is also recognized, poetically, that this quality, this character or persona, is not their fault. One speaks of the 'loose loincloth being unprotective' and thereby being the cause; hence the saying, *Afwong'o jang'uono* ('loincloth the generous one').

In opposition to the discourses about sexuality, about the 'society of the grass' in Siaya, the young men of Kaloleni in Nairobi perceive Siaya to be full of 'upright girls'. When the men of Kaloleni are ready to marry, they assure themselves, the chaste girls described in their grandfathers' lessons will be available to them, as opposed to the 'loose and shop-worn girls' of Kaloleni among whom they move rather freely. The girls of Kaloleni regard Siaya as being full of young bumpkins; they call their country age mates by the Swahili slang term *miro*; the young of the country are thought to know nothing about sexuality or about life. The young of Siaya see Kaloleni as a place where sexuality is about money, something you pay for or are paid for, where the girls are spoiled: *okethore*.

Women commonly evaluate men through an aesthetic of labour, which concerns the forms, qualities, values, and statuses of work. Certain jobs were clearly despised by Siaya folk. One can look back through several decades at such critical expression. One of the richest contexts for observations are songs that have gained popularity in Siaya. This *magenge* song, sung by girls in the early 1950s, illustrates one such job description: the farm labourer.

> Achayo nae Jasamba
> Achayo nae Jasamba
> Jotich Karaya
> Achayo nae Jasamba.
>
> (I despise the labourer
> I despise the labourer
> Carriers of Karais
> I despise the labourers.)

The *magenge* (*ondoro*) girls sang another song which mocked the clothing typically worn by agricultural workers in Kenya. In a song competition in 1953, Jennifer's Liganua Ondoro team sang,

> Yawuoyi ma twang'ire gi
> Sat Okinda
> Yawuoyi ma twang'ire gi
> Sat Okinda
> Mago Wachayo.
>
> (The boys who purchase
> blue-striped shirts
> The boys who purchase
> blue-striped shirts
> Those we
> despise.)

It is commonly stated by Luo in both the city and the countryside that the town is disruptive of marital peace and family stability. Also appreciated is the fact that the ultimate loser in the break-up of a marriage is the husband's mother. That is so because the son's wife, left in the village, is her helper in old age. This is particularly so because on the average she would be a widow, as women marry younger and outlive their husbands by a decade or two, or more. Hence the admonishing beer song that is popular in Aram market in Asembo:

> Ee meru ogumni
> Ka chiegi oa
> Kiwuotho gi Amina
> Nyar Miji
> Ma Hm Hm Hm.
>
> (Lo, your mother may streak.
> When your wife deserts you
> For hanging out with Amina
> A town girl
> Who is . . . [unmentionable].)

Sometimes Paulina lay awake thinking about it. The district was quiet enough with its big gardens and widely spaced houses, and yet these days it never seemed quiet to a woman who had endured the sounds of eight households mingling over the wooden rafters of Pumwani or the noise of sacks and boxes swaying perilously overhead in Kariokor and latecomers squeezing past folded chairs and unrolled mats in adjacent rooms. Here dogs barked at night suspiciously, on the defence rather than on heat, and, human noise being caged in protective houses or convoyed out in automobiles to vent its passion elsewhere, the distant sounds of traffic hung long in the air, like the early morning bus at home that was heard so far off, amid the unmechanical buzz of night, that you could get up and dress and be ready to catch it at the market.[14]

'The boat is a bride'

The Uyoma peninsula is a gently rolling terrain that constitutes a boundary between the waters of the Winam Gulf and the large and often stormy seas of Lake Victoria. Katweng'a is one settlement among many in Uyoma whose inhabitants take advantage of the waterside location to engage not only in farming but also in lake-borne enterprise and fishing.

From March until August or September, the people of Katweng'a are preoccupied with gardening, weeding, and harvesting of millet and some maize. By October, the harvests are done and like many other communities in Yimbo, Uyoma, and Asembo, the people turn their attention to the lake, spending the next four or five months at the lakeshore, or on the lake.

Nets are set in the evening and the catch brought in early in the morning. By nine in the morning the villages empty out and men, women, and children go to the lakeshore where they meet, exchange ideas, buy and sell, wash, swim, and mend their boats and their fishing nets.

The fishing boat is central to the Katweng'a world.[15] The construction of the vessel begins with the selection, by the contractor, or boat owner to be, of a ten or twelve metre-long post called *migongo*. This is the keel of the vessel and the contractor takes the post to the carpenter, who will complete the construction.

The *migongo* is fixed to the ground by use of pegs (*loch*) and four other poles (*mberni*) of the same length as the keel are brought to the construction ground along the shore. Two of these posts (*awasi*) are set above the keel, one on each side. The two other posts (*aluop*) are each cut into six pieces, and are set above the *awasi* so that crossbars can be inserted at intervals as seats. Two carved pieces of wood are fixed fore and aft for use in piloting. A pilot's seat, *rahum*, is installed. The stern is carved into a beak as an insignia, as identification; and the horns of an animal, either *ngau* or *nyakech*, are hung over the beak, the horns facing backwards. Spaces between the posts are filled in and the vessel made watertight by use of cork, lime, pieces or iron, and cotton wool.

The launching (*nyasi*) of a new boat in Uyoma is a major event, a time of festivity and sociability, and also a time of reverence, meaning, and ritual moments. There are several of these ritual moments: there is the rebirth of the *jok*, the controlling spirit force, after whom the boat has been named; there is an appeal to the *jok* and to the spirits of the lake to accept the boat as worthy; and there is the handing over of the boat, as a 'bride' — for so it has been referred to throughout the planning and construction of the vessel — to the 'groom'.

It is most common to name a new boat after a married daughter, *migogo*, and it is as a daughter of the homestead that the boat is treated; hence the expression 'Yie en migogo' ('a boat — *yie* — is a married daughter').

At the time when a boat assumes a name, and one speaks of the boat assuming a name rather than people giving a boat a name, the boat becomes wild. The boat must be tamed, adopted, socialized, so that it may be put to daily use. It is said that *jok lango* has entered the vessel ('*yie alokore jalango*') and that it is unsafe to take it on to the water. Wild, the vessel might drown a person. The taming or socialization process is called *riso*, which is also used within the marriage ceremony.

The boat appears to the owner in a dream (sometimes to his wife or a relative) and gives direction as to the exact manner in which the *jok* would like it to be launched, i.e. the day, the time, the exact place, who is going to be the spiritual mother (*Omwasi* or *Nyamrech*, as she is called); and whether *riso* and *rwako*, the process of welcoming it as a daughter of the village are both to take place on the same day. Sometimes the boat may demand that *rwako* should come before *riso*, but generally *riso* is the earlier process.

On the specified day for *riso*, Omwasi, who is usually a sister-in-law to the boat

owner, brings along with her the following items:
1. *Odheru*, a grass-woven tray. It must be new and must not be one already smeared with cowdung.
2. Grains of maize, grains of millet, grains of simsim, grains of finger-millet; ghee, groundnuts, cowpeas, beans, and bananas.

These are the traditional gifts a step-mother gives to her step-daughter on the day of the latter's marriage. The boat ... is at this stage treated as a bride. In addition, the *Omwasi* cooks a pottage (*ugali*) of simsim, finger millet, and ghee. This pottage is carried into the boat, as well as other gifts like:

Men's earrings, feathers of a cock for plumes, bangles, *dol* (this is the tail of a species of wildcat known as *kaki* or *ng'unydeng'*). These last are presents which a bride takes to her husband on the day of marriage.[16]

There are at least two launchings of the vessel. At the first, the spiritual father of the vessel, who has been selected by the person who has contracted the boat's construction, and the contractor pour a libation of beer to the *jok* or spirit of the vessel. Then the builder cuts the ropes that fasten the keel to the ground. This is a critical moment, for the cutting of the bindings releases the *jok* of the vessel into the world of living beings. Then the contractor carefully cleanses the boat of spells (*dino juok*), which enemies may have placed in the boat to harm the owner or the vessel. When this is done, the onlookers move forward and push the boat into the water stern first, and then it is turned around and given a test run and then it is returned to shore.

For this second 'launching', the spiritual mother (*Omwasi*) of the vessel boards the boat. Accompanied by a good deal of ululation, she presents the *jok* of the boat with the gifts that she had earlier brought down to the shore; *odheru*, the tray with grains of various kinds, groundnuts, bananas, ghee, cowpeas, beans, and simsim. This is the culmination of the process called *riso*, which began with the preparations for the launching. It is the *Omwasi* who, after presenting these gifts, goes out into the lake in the boat, yelling and ululating. It is this supreme act of hers, this ululation, that is called *riso yie*. She continues to ululate while the boat is in competition with the others. On return to shore she presents the *jok* with the second set of gifts: beads, men's earrings, plumes, bangles, *dol* (the tail of *kaki*, a wildcat).

As the husband is anxious to start a home of his own and cannot do so while his wife is constantly running back to her parents he now pays the cattle as fast as he can. When he has paid from six to twelve head of cattle he sends his *jagam*, the go-between who negotiated the marriage, with his brothers to tell his father-in-law that he has now paid the bridewealth and wants the *riso* ceremony to be held. He says that he will pay later the cattle still owing. After this ceremony his wife will remain with him and be a full wife to him in both a domestic and legal sense. She will cook for him and he will have redress if she has sexual intercourse with other men in the *simba*. The *riso* is the binding act of marriage.[17]

With a good deal of enthusiasm, onlookers come forward and

present gifts by placing them in the boat: goats, money, baskets, fruit. This is the final act of the drama of *riso*, which has as its object the taming of the *lango* or *juogi* of the boat. It is only after the completion of *riso* that there is a possibility of the *jok* of the boat being at peace with other and contrary spiritual forces. The boat is considered lakeworthy.

There is but one more ritual to be completed before the new vessel assumes the day-to-day activity of the other boats. This is *rwako*. Here again, it is said that the *jok* of the vessel appears to the owner and briefs him on the precise gifts it would prefer and concerning the details of the ritual, which will bring the 'bride' into the family and homestead of the owner. The gifts might be a cock of a particular colour selected by the *jok*, a male goat of a particular colour selected by the *jok*, and beer.

Throughout the rituals of launching, people speak of the 'bride', the boat, being brought home to her parents. A feast is finally organized in her honour. The feast for the new boat is called *dwoko*, which is also the feast for the bride in the marriage ceremony.

The construction and launching of a boat is one continuous series of acts of worship and reverence. The new vessel is personified, a specific *juogi* is identified with it, and guides its construction and the rituals for its protection. The new vessel is also a bride, and is welcomed home and adopted as one of the family (*rwako*) after the *juogi* have been tamed through the work of *riso*.

There are other ways in which the spirit forces associated with the boat reveal themselves and require mediation. If a boatman of a vessel dies out in the lake, the boat signals tragedy to the people on shore by returning stern first. Such a death is considered an extreme tragedy, as if one had killed a kinsman. The *jok* of a boat is blamed for this, and the boat has therefore to be cleansed once again. This cleansing is called *gudo yie* or *dino yie*. For this, a black ram, a cockerel, and medicinal ashes are used. An exorcist speaks to the offending *jok* and berates it, reprimanding it for the bad deed. What is noted is that there is a recognition that the same *jok* has good and bad, protective and dangerous, powers. In their malevolent guise they may be termed *jochiende*. Those who died in the water are buried by the lake. It would invite danger to bury such dead in the homestead. Similarly, if the boatmen pick a corpse out of the water, it is never taken into the boat, but is tied by a rope and towed into shore.

In Uyoma, dreams referring to boats and their *jok* are commonly discussed. A boat may appear to the owner, or to his wife, or to the spiritual mother (*Omwasi*) in a vision or a dream. It is said that on such occasions the *jok* of the boat speaks, while the person sees the boat. It is said that the boat comes to warn of an impending disaster or a significant future event. Sometimes the *jok* may demand, through a dream or vision, that an offering or sacrifice be made on its behalf; sometimes the owner witnesses the whole impending drama enacted on the boat. People say that in these pre-enactments no voices may actually be heard. In cases where the boat is named after an ancestor, the ancestor may choose the boat to be his or her medium of communication with the boat owner. It is also said that when a boat is stolen, it may appear to the owner in a dream and let him know from whom and where it may be recovered.

The journey of the *jogam*

One of the problems for Adhiambo's husband was that he had been rather remiss in visiting his wife's home and in arranging for friends to visit Adhiambo's family to settle the marriage. The young husband was a teacher and one of his excuses was that he had been transferred several times. His transfers had meant that he and Adhiambo had lived together for only a few months since they had declared their marriage nearly three years before. Adhiambo wrote weekly, pleading for her husband to arrange for the marriage settlement and to take her away to live with him. Adhiambo's pleas reached her husband's comrades in Boro and they too began to pressure the husband to complete his marriage responsibilities. Eventually the husband visited Boro and met with his friends. He gave them a thousand shillings to 'go and settle the marriage' as soon as possible. 'It was unlikely,' he said, 'that I will be able to pay any more than that.'

The comrades sent messages ahead to Adhiambo that they, the *jogam*, were coming the following Saturday; they said that they were certain they could settle everything; and that she could leave with them to return to Boro.

It was a 40km trip by road to Yimbo Majengo and it was not difficult for the *jogam* — Elijah, Nashon, Daudi, and Ochanda — to reach Adhiambo's home by car. Elijah later recalled:[18]

'We were greeted by Adhiambo's sister Edwina who took us into their Mother's house. We were seated on the northern side of the room following the arrangement of our forefathers, facing the southern side, where the mothers and fathers-in-law sat when they came in to greet us and to chat. On our side were the brothers and sisters of Adhiambo, the bride. Adhiambo took a position on the eastern side of the house near the door. Once *103*

we were seated we were greeted steadily by a considerable progress of Adhiambo's people and neighbours. Adhiambo's actual
father came and greeted us but then excused himself as "he had
important things to take care of". We were told that his elder
brother would take care of us in his absence.'

Tea was brought and was taken with the sub-chief of the location, who happened to be related to Adhiambo. After tea,
Adhiambo's uncle entered and there was talk about Yimbo, about
the condition of the cattle and the farms in the area, about the
rains. The uncle left and a portable record player was brought
in and some music was played while lunch was served.

After lunch the sub-chief's father came in with some female
relations of Adhiambo and they asked a number of questions
concerning the backgrounds of the *jogam*. Sodas and *chang'aa* were
brought and served and beer and cigarettes offered.

After a few drinks, the sub-chief came in and sat down. After
a few minutes of whispering with the older women in the room,
he turned to Adhiambo and began to harangue her:

'If these 'brothers-in-law' are weak, we are going to chase them
away, but before we do you better just show us the actual brother-
in-law present. Who are these people? Are they really brothers-
in-law? Our women here are complaining bitterly that since these
jogam arrived they haven't greeted our people properly.
Adhiambo and her sisters here are young and shy.'

The father of the sub-chief then asked a riddle: 'Shyness barred
a hare from . . . ?' And Ochanda started to speak but was
stranded. Adhiambo's sister helped: '. . . from coming out of
its hiding place.'

The sub-chief then moved on to the point at hand:

'If you have not produced the proper greetings, then how about
when it will come to the time when the mothers-in-law of your
groom will demand their alcohol, and then the boys, and then
the old people will ask . . . and then we will confiscate your car,
move it behind the house, and use it for drying cassava. Before
you blink, your car will be a hill of cassava.'

Nashon responded: 'Go and take the car then . . . ' and this
seemed to have the effect of driving the sub-chief out of the house.

Elijah wondered quietly to the brothers of Adhiambo, 'What
hostility! Does it mean that nobody has ever come here since
these two people got married?' The answer, in brief, was that
no one had come. 'We are the first people,' added Nashon, 'and
they were married in 1976.' Elijah groaned, 'There are going
to be a lot of problems . . . We will have to do the best we can,
but in the end we will have to write to _____ and tell
him the situation is pretty bad.'

The sub-chief came back in and turned on the visitors, 'The mothers-in-law have said that you have not greeted them; you haven't greeted the fathers-in-law either, nor the boys, nor the sisters-in-law, and just bear in mind that since you came here some time ago all you have been doing is drinking and eating bare the home of your hosts.' Ochanda responded angrily, 'We haven't seen anything but abuse so we have nothing to thank you people for.'

The sub-chief tried a different line: 'You must know that Alego and Yimbo are quite different and therefore everything is going to be conducted here according to our liking, not yours; we have no interest in your arguments.' Ochanda then replied, 'For our part, we will proceed according to how the Alego people do it because we are totally ignorant of how you conduct things here in Yimbo and it looks like we will get no help from you in understanding the differences between Yimbo and Alego.'

The sub-chief:

'Why haven't you asked Adhiambo how things are done in Yimbo? After all you have been involved in this marriage for more than three years. This shows that you are both stupid and dishonest . . . Adhiambo, tell your "dear" brothers-in-law to put their car on the road and get some *chang'aa* from Nyamonye market, or is it in that immense boot . . . and why did they bring that car here . . . to show it off . . . or for us to dry our cassava?'

The visitors went out to the car and discussed what had happened over the first three hours at Adhiambo's home. They spent about fifteen minutes deciding whether fifty or two hundred shillings (of their comrade's one thousand) would have to be put down on the table right away as a 'greeting'. On the one hand there was the feeling that all that they needed to pay for was the alcohol because they could not be expected to pay for the food and tea; on the other hand there was a fear that their hosts would swallow the two hundred shillings and make further demands before even proceeding to the negotiations of the bridewealth. Ochanda argued forcefully that 'These people have been testing our minds and if they discover any weakness they can play with our minds and we will find that we have given out a lot of money for nothing. First, we have to be careful about the drinks and try to keep our heads straight. And even if one of us makes a mistake, we must not give in.'

The *jogam* resumed their seats in the house, a basin of water was brought in for washing of hands before eating, and the food was brought in. The sub-chief then put on a very serious face and turned to the women: 'Return the food to the kitchen, we cannot feed people whom we don't know, where we don't know whence they came, and where we cannot even see a cow in the vicinity. These young people don't seem to know that visitors help the owner of the home.' He then turned to Ochanda and asked, 'Now you don't know whether or not we want you to pay for your food with money and you cannot figure this out just by looking around?'

Elijah tried to change the flow of conversation:

'We have been under self-control here and we have proceeded by the standards of practice in Alego, but you want us to do it at the same time in the Yimbo way, which is impossible. You raise the question of cattle, but know that that is out because your cows around here are never looked after . . . they just roam around the bush and aren't brought home even in two days.'

The sub-chief responded, 'Can't you see the tethering poles just out there? . . . Maybe you don't know the use of those poles. When we settled an Alego family who gave us a girl she told us not to shame her but only to produce what we had.'

As the sub-chief's wife and Adhiambo started to serve the food, Ochanda remarked that

'We did not come to eat, if you feel that we are your visitors who are worth providing for, then feed us, but if you feel that we are not worth providing for, then don't feed us. We haven't asked for food, and, after all, since we came here we have seen nobody we recognize as sisters-in-law and mothers-in-law.'

The food was eaten slowly, with some flirting between the *jogam* and the sisters of Adhiambo and some jokes passed back and forth with the brothers. Drinks were brought and the sub-chief came in again. Ochanda asked for the actual people of Adhiambo to come in . . . 'We have something for the uncle and the mother of Adhiambo. We do not want to give it to the sub-chief.' The uncle came in and Ochanda handed him some cash, folded into a tight bundle. The uncle unfolded it, laid it on the table and slowly counted it. 'My friends,' he said, 'They have brought us thirty shillings.' And then he handed it to the sub-chief.

Ochanda tried to control his anger.

'We once more thank you for the entertainments we have had since we came here . . . I think our visit was not an abrupt one . . . we sent proper notice in advance . . . and we hope you expected us . . . our main aim of coming was to arrange for Adhiambo to go back to her husband. We have come to take Adhiambo and whatever has to be done we will do in the morning and then we will leave. But now we are tired.'

The sub-chief erupted: 'How can you want Adhiambo, yet since you came here . . . you haven't produced a shilling or a calf . . . you haven't produced anything to show that you want her . . . and then there is the matter of the child . . . it stays here with Adhiambo and is fed by us.' The father of the sub-chief added, 'The small thing that you have brought for us, just put it on the table now, so that if it is very small then we will criticize you here and now before you go to sleep.' The sub-chief added, 'If it is indeed small, then we will pack you in your car right away . . . without the cassava . . . and off you go.'

Elijah replied, 'According to our plan, we wanted to leave with Adhiambo tomorrow and whatever small thing that we have brought shall be produced tomorrow at our departure time.'

The sub-chief exploded,

'Who is this child who does not know how to talk? We have never seen a person who goes to pay bridewealth and leaves the cow out of the home and says that he will bring the cow tomorrow when he departs. I suppose you are going to throw money at us tomorrow and then run away before we count it. Even if your cow is very thin, just produce it now and even if it is money, just place it on the table so that we can count it now. If you really knew what was going on and if you knew how to speak, child, you would have told us that our daughter is not staying here properly.'

Ochanda tried to respond to the new wrinkle, about which he had only just been made aware by Nashon: 'Mzee, our coming here should show you that we want our wife back, but as she left her husband only she knows the cause, and we do not know it. We are not so stupid that we would "walk" all this distance from Boro with empty hands.'

The subchief: 'Adhiambo isn't able to talk because if she does you will assume that we have made her say things . . . just produce the small thing you have brought . . . that is what we want.'

The father of the sub-chief: 'The cow, whether it is lean or not, has to be tethered in the centre of the home so that if it is useless, you can be abused for your cheapness right here and now and if it is a good one you can be praised straightaway. Therefore, whatever you've brought, just produce it whether it is but a five cent piece.'

Elijah then added, 'The fact that we shall give you the money tomorrow does not mean that we shall produce the money and then run away, because in fact we have to learn about Adhiambo's situation before we leave with her.'

Elijah, Nashon, and Daudi then excused themselves and went to the car to get the rest of the money and while they were outside discussing their progress, the sub-chief abused Ochanda for bringing fools and idiots who did nothing but sneak around counting money since they arrived in the morning (it was by then night).

The positions were resumed and Nashon handed the sub-chief a packet of bills folded tightly. The packet was handed around, with each elder asking another to count it. The uncle slowly counted the money and announced that it was 'nine hundred and ninety'. Elijah asked for a recount and the sub-chief slowly counting aloud again reached one thousand. Then the sub-chief spoke:

'I have never seen a case where people came to pay bridewealth before an "agreement fee" was paid and before the "food fee" was paid . . . therefore let us divide this money up and see what is left as bridewealth. Even if you boys think that this thousand shillings should be kept as one, maybe all that will remain as bridewealth will be five bob . . . and then Adhiambo's husband will have to settle the rest before we proceed with these negotiations.'

There was a lengthy discussion about the differences in practice between Alego and Yimbo in the disposition of marriage payments. Finally, the uncle conceded that the funds would be treated as bridewealth in their entirety.

The record-player was brought back to the room and there was music and dancing, with a good deal of teasing and joking between the *jogam* and Adhiambo's people. Eventually, the gathering broke up and the visitors were shown sleeping places in one of the houses in the compound. Before going to sleep, Daudi, Nashon, Elijah, and Ochanda discussed the long day's negotiation and felt that they had done well for their comrade, Adhiambo's husband.

The next morning breakfast was served in Adhiambo's mother's house and the mother spoke up for the first time:

'I really had hope in Atieno's father [that is, the groom, Adhiambo's husband — Atieno was Adhiambo's young daughter]. But now I have lost hope in him completely, because since Adhiambo married him he has not written to us once and since Adhiambo came back from him two months ago he has not even written to Adhiambo or anyone else here to find out about Adhiambo's whereabouts. The father of Atieno is a person whose behaviour we know too well. Ever since he took Adhiambo three years ago we have not asked him for anything . . . a poor person pays bridewealth with his eyes. The fathers of Adhiambo's husband have not come here either and show that they are also useless . . . neither have they written. With me I have no problem . . . when writing to Atieno's father tell him that his mother-in-law wanted to smack the *jogam* because he was not here himself to take the punishment that he deserves.'

As they went to their car, Adhiambo, with Atieno at her side, came over and said that she would not leave now, but would wait for word from her husband. Except for this small group, the compound was empty. The journey back to Boro was a long one.

A young man wishing to marry will ask a *jagam* or intermediary to find a wife for him. The *jagam* is usually a 'father's sister', a 'father's sister's son' or a 'mother's brother', all of whom reside in communities other than that of the bridegroom; or the *jagam* may be a 'brother's wife' who has links to her natal community. This *jagam* will approach the girl and her parents. If they are agreeable, the *jagam* will then arrange a meeting between the prospective bride and groom.[19]

As the husband is anxious to start a home of his own and cannot do so while his wife is constantly running back to her parents he now pays the cattle as fast as he can. When he has paid from six to twelve head of cattle he sends the *jagam*, the go-between who negotiated the marriage, with his brothers, to tell his father-in-law that he has now paid the bridewealth and wants the *riso* ceremony to be held. He says that he will pay later the cattle still owing. After this ceremony his wife will remain with him and be a full wife to him in both a domestic and legal sense. The *riso* is the binding act of marriage ... When the *jagam* and the husband's brothers make their request the wife's people laugh at them: 'What are twelve (maybe) head of cattle? You are playing a game. You can go and tell your brother to come and take his cattle back.' The *jagam* refuses to make any more payments, so they tell him to go back and tell his friend to remove his cattle ... The *jagam* and the father argue. Everyone knows more or less what is going to happen.[20]

NOTES

1. Betty Potash, 'Marriage stability in a rural Luo community', *Africa*, 48,4 (1978) p.388. For further discussion of marriage, see E.E. Evans-Pritchard, 'Marriage customs of the Luo of Kenya', in E.E. Evans-Pritchard, *The Position of Women in Primitive Societies and Other Essays in Social Anthropology* (New York, The Free Press, 1965), pp.228-44 (originally published in *Africa*, 20, 2 (1950), pp.132-42); and Simeon H. Ominde, *The Luo Girl From Infancy to Marriage* (Nairobi, East African Literature Bureau, 1952); and Michael Whisson, *Change and Challenge: A Study of the Social and Economic Changes among the Kenya Luo* (Nairobi, National Christian Council of Kenya, 1964).
2. Margaret Jean Hay has discussed the role of Luo women in the colonial economy: 'Luo women and economic change during the colonial period', in Nancy J. Hafkin and Edna G. Bay (eds), *Women in Africa: Studies in Social and Economic Change* (Stanford, Stanford University Press, 1976), pp.87-109.
3. Potash, 'Marriage stability', p.395.
4. It might be remarked here that Luo lineage histories present the patrilineages as being founded around 'autonomous' female figures.
5. Some observers say that the practice of injection is helping to spread the AIDS virus through western Kenya.
6. Grace Ogot, *The Promised Land* (Nairobi, East African Publishing House, 1966), p.134.
7. Oginga Odinga, *Not Yet Uhuru: An Autobiography* (New York, Hill & Wang, 1969), p.10.
8. From communication provided by Elijah Oduor Ogutu, following discussions with elderly women who had been brought up by a *pim*. There has been little research published on *pim* and the *siwindhe*, but see A. B. C. Ocholla-Ayayo, *Traditional Ideology and Ethics among the Southern Luo*

(Uppsala, Scandinavian Institute of African Studies, 1976), pp.73-4: also, David William Cohen, 'Pim's work: some thoughts on the construction of relations and groups — the Luo of western Kenya', paper presented to a conference on 'The History of the Family in Africa', School of Oriental and African Studies, London, September, 1981; and A. B. Odaga, 'Some aspects of the Luo traditional education transmitted through the oral narratives — *sigendini*'. UNESCO Seminar on Oral Traditions, Past Growth and Future Development in East Africa, Kisumu, April, 1979, pp.4-7. Ocholla-Ayayo and Odaga see the *siwindhe* as an important setting for the transmission of oral narratives, *sigendini*, in the past, under the tutelage of *pim*.

9. Some older Luo have related that widows without protection were occasionally seized and sacrificed to assure the well-being of a new Lake Victoria transport or fishing craft.

10. Whisson, *Change and Challenge*, p.24.

11. 'Muzungu' was not the Luo word for a European or a person of another culture but is, rather, a Bantu term drawn jokingly into Luo parlance. Granny is not so much an adaptation of English references to 'Grannies' or 'Nannies' but seems, rather, simply a Luo speech play on her knowledge of European ways.

12. Ben G. Blount, 'Aspects of Luo socialization', *Language and Society*, 1 (1979), pp.247-8.

13. This discussion of *pim* is adapted from David William Cohen, 'Doing social history from *pim*'s doorway', in Olivier Zunz (ed.), *Reliving the Past: The Worlds of Social History* (Chapel Hill, University of North Carolina Press, 1985), pp.191-6. Most of the testimonies which we have collected about *pim* focus on the instruction concerning sexuality and sexual practice within and outside marriage.

14. Marjorie Oludhe Macgoye, *Coming to Birth* (Nairobi, Heinemann, 1986), p.108.

15. This discussion of the construction and launching of an Uyoma fishing vessel is drawn from E. S. Atieno Odhiambo, 'Some aspects of religious activity among the Uyoma fishermen: the rites connected with the launching of a fishing vessel', *Mila*, 1, 2 (1970), pp.14-21. For an excellent treatment of lake-borne trade in the region see Michael G. Kenny, 'Precolonial trade in eastern Lake Victoria', *Azania*, 14 (1979), pp.97-107.

16. Odhiambo, 'Aspects of religious activity' pp.16-17.

17. Evans-Pritchard, 'Marriage customs', p.235.

18. The account of the trip to settle Adhiambo's bridewealth was prepared from notes written down by Elijah Oduor Ogutu and David William Cohen soon after the trip. The *jogam* stayed at Yimbo Majengo for a little more than twenty-four hours; it was quite impossible to recount the entire negotiation, given the density of the conversation and the multiplicity of voices. Perhaps forty persons from Adhiambo's family and neighbourhood participated in the negotiation.

19. Potash, 'Marriage stability' pp.381-2.

20. Evans-Pritchard, 'Marriage customs', p.235.

An Anthropology of the Shadows VI

In late 1985, one of the authors of the present work received a letter from a former research assistant, an employee of the National Museums of Kenya. He reported that he had been doing some research in the collections of the museum and had come across a series of photographs taken in western Kenya around 1900. He wrote, 'The pictures were a shock to see. They show us naked as the day we were born, naked, without any clothes. I can't believe that we Luo went about naked and without shame.'

The photographs in question were taken around the time that the idea of wearing clothing was catching on fast in the region of Siaya. The pacification campaigns in western Kenya, organized by the Imperial British East Africa Company (IBEAC) and later the British station at Mumias, brought Nubian troops into the area, and their numbers were bolstered as efforts were made to put down Nandi resistance. The growth of British and allied forces in western Kenya created employment opportunities for the people of the area, as well as introducing new styles of dress. With the construction of the railway, still more opportunities for employment became available. Men from the Siaya area went for employment in order to obtain cloth and clothing.

Three men, Petro Nyamgero, Owor Pando, and Atieno ka Oyugi left the village of Liganua in Siaya, took employment with the Nubian soldiers and were the first to bring clothes to Liganua.[1] Atieno brought a *kanzu* to his father Oyugi, as well as a red blanket referred to in those days as *baranged* (blanket) *kiboko*. Because these people brought clothes they were referred to as *jonanga*, the people of clothes. Some of those who went for employment might be appropriately characterized as 'target workers', people who came to work for a fixed material object and then went back home. But it is important to note that there were also 'career workers', people who spent most of their lives working outside their village areas. And this phenomenon of the

111

career worker was as old as colonialism itself.[2]

One such career belonged to Atieno Oyugi, the pioneer of the red blanket. Between 1899 and 1901 he worked for the Nubians in Koru. The year 1902 found him in Elureko, where again he worked for the Nubians, adopted Nubian dress and behaviour, spoke Swahili and Arabic, and was referred to as Mungwana. Atieno was in the Turkana expedition of 1904-5, fighting with the British levies, and at the conclusion of the expedition went to work in Lumbwa for a settler known as Bwana Rabala. He was baptized as Stefano in the period between 1905 and 1908. The First World War years found him working again in Koru, this time for Conway Harvey, the notorious settler leader of this area. It was in Koru that he spent the rest of his life, working for settlers like Pattimore and Down (Bwana Obam). In 1924 he went to work for Ismael Smith (Bwana Debe) at Oduwo, and was promoted to a supervisory position in 1925. Atieno worked on the same farm for thirteen years, until his death in 1938, also serving Bwana Allen, who bought the farm from Ismael Smith.

The significance of the biography of Atieno of Liganua is that it draws attention to the pattern of career service among Siaya folk, going back to the beginning of the century. Atieno was one among many who left their homes for long and short periods in order to acquire material wealth and to bring back what were perceived as positive and useful notions from the outside. These individuals came to be referred to as *jopango*. They served as crucial communicators of culture into Liganua and hundreds of other neighbourhoods in western Kenya.

Jopango brought back material goods other than cloth: *sufurias* (saucepans), *karais* (basins), *jembes* (hoes). Sufurias and karais in particular were the kind of items *jopango* obtained through working for the railway. Ogunia and jembes were items most commonly obtained through working for settlers on their farms. The inflow of material goods was slow at first, but increased steadily as the numbers of *jopango* grew.

Important ideas were associated with the *jopango*, with *pango*. There was, first, the idea of distance, of travelling a distance to a new place of work, *kapango* (the place of work). The *kapango* was somewhere far, 'upcountry', *malo*. *Kapango* was also the place where clothes, *kananga*, came from, and those who came back and took to wearing clothes were called *jonanga*. It was the kind of place where one met the *mzungu*, so it was also called *Kawasungu*. The *mzungu* was the foreigner, the European, and while in some areas of eastern Africa this term could take on a negative connotation, in Liganua the cognitive reaction to the *mzungu* presence was positive. The *mzungu* was spoken of in Liganua as *ombogo jarachar* (the white man), *odiero wuod lando* (the blue-eyed son of the light-skinned girl), *apala palo wuoth* (the grey man with a strange gait).

Some of the habits of the *mzungu* were little understood in Liganua, and were not copied or borrowed, but were admired all the same, like his lying in state fully dressed before burial. In terms of superlative reference, the *mzungu* became the man of culture *par excellence*, the one to whom all deferred, the subject of so much conversation at the places of employment and back in Liganua. You dressed well like a *mzungu*, or you spoke English well like a *mzungu*, or even if you spoke Dholuo particularly distinctively, you were said to speak like a *mzungu*.

The particular 'species' of *mzungu* that caught the imagination of the people of Liganua in the 1920s and 1930s was the Scotsman. The most polished of *jonanga* in the 1930s was Okola ka Yewa. His more popular name was Okola Skoch. One can cite other examples of the incorporation of the other and the distant into the everyday discourse of Liganua. The name of the well-known leader of the settlers, and enormously successful dairy farmer, Lord Delamere found currency in Liganua. A certain Okoth Ka Opiyo, an Uhanya man, used to be Delamere's herdboy, one of many, in the 1920s. When he returned home to Siaya he arranged to supply two bottles of milk a day to an Indian shopkeeper at Ndere (just across the Rabolo river from Liganua). The Indian, Govindji Karsandas Karia, was known locally as Ogonji. Because Okoth could supply milk all year round and be paid for it by Ogonji, the analogy was that he was doing as well as Delamere. He therefore acquired the name of Okoth Ouro Dalmia (Delamere).

The distant and complex figure of Lord Delamere was an idea introduced into Liganua through *jopango*. Whatever the conditions of work on the Delamere estate may have been, it was the positive aspect that gained currency in the neighbourhood of Liganua. The example indicates that the process of communication centred on the *jopango* could be far more *subtle* than simply adopting European material goods. And these discussions centring on the *jopango* included notions, discussed above, concerning the distinctions between opportunities in Uganda and those 'in Kenya'.

Another element that came into Liganua in the same period was the idea of playing tennis. The servants of the *mzungu* saw him dress in white, wear a scarf and 'turkeys' (tennis shoes), take his racquet and tennis balls, and go to the tennis court. By the time the idea of tennis reached Liganua, the sequence had been revised a bit. Wilson Oluoch Oton, who was employed on a European farm as a cook, bought tennis clothes and a tennis racquet, came home on holidays and would take an afternoon walk through Liganua in this uniform, not playing the game, just exercising his hands and arms swinging the racquet. The idea caught on, and others in Liganua did the same. Similarly, in the 1940s, men like Okech Oraro Kobambo would dress in full coat and tails, and then go to Siaya Market and play golf in the mid-day sun on market day.

The aesthetics of Liganua were also changing. The older concept of the beautiful girl, one with a long neck, was partially displaced. By the 1940s, Othieno Odiemo, a much travelled *jopango*, was talking about beauty in Liganua in terms of *kwar ka nyar Goa* (being brown like a Goan girl) or *ber ka nya Silisili* (being as beautiful as a Seychelloise).

The *jopango* were brokers among cultures and their effect on life in Liganua was enormous. There was also another reference group, the *josomo*, the readers. Western education had an early impact on Liganua, specifically through the appearance of Christianity in the neighbourhood. The local 'agent' of the expansion of the *josomo* was James Lucas Oganga. In 1902, Jemsi, as he was known and as he is remembered, went to visit Atieno at his work place at Elureko, and stayed with him there. The year 1904 found Jemsi in Nairobi with Mariko Abwao. They were employed at the Norfolk Hotel. Later, Jemsi worked for Sir Northrup MacMillan as a gun bearer. He joined the Bible School run by Canon Burns in 1910, and was baptized in 1912. When war broke out in East Africa in 1914, Jemsi went home and joined John Paul Olola at Nyadhi, where the latter had built a church. In 1917, Jemsi left Nyadhi and went to Liganua. On 7 March 1917, the first Liganua Church was built.

Jemsi became an agent for new ideas in a very fundamental sense. For a start, he put on white shorts, which were kept impeccably clean. Second, he smoked a Western pipe. Third, Jemsi built himself a homestead by his church, the first bachelor in the area ever to build a homestead. Jemsi therefore attracted the attention of his age-mates, some of whom were attracted by his innovations in Liganua while others spurned him as a lost soul. It is not clear how Jemsi's support gathered about him, or just why others showed revulsion towards him. What is clear is that Jemsi had no governmental backing for his ventures, and no material rewards to give out to his followers. Thus, those who came forward to his church appear to have come in freely. Among the many who joined him were Eba Aloo chi Mwalo, Lois Opang'a chi Mwalo, Flora Awich chi Omolo, and Sofia Oloo chi Sihaya.

In turn, these women set up what they and those around them recognized as the 'first Christian homes' in Liganua. They brought their children to Church, had them baptized, and raised them to 'fear the Lord'. Jemsi taught these children reading, writing, and arithmetic in Dholuo in the class he held every afternoon. These were mixed classes, and after a while some of the girls under Jemsi's teaching were married and carried their *josomo* orientation to other parts of the country.

Perhaps the greatest single innovation after the building of Jemsi's Liganua Church was the establishment of a 'Church Village', known as *laini*, around the Church at Liganua. What happened was that Jemsi invited some of his age-mates to leave their father's homesteads and join him near the Church. Here they built rectangular houses (*od kibanda*) as opposed to the older round huts, and they lived according to Christian precepts.

All through the 1920s and 1930s the *laini* prospered, finding great inspiration from Beseba nyar Ogonya, Jemsi's wife, with whom Jemsi celebrated the first Christian wedding in the area in 1923. Beseba developed a reputation as a great hymnalist, and in her prime she taught the women how to sing in tonic solfa, and how to sew. The Christian community in Liganua was very much encouraged by the late Reverend George Samwel Okoth, who from 1925 was the local pastor, and also by Archdeacon Owen of Maseno and Reverend Pleydell (Bwana Orengo) of Ngiya. Many people came to Liganua to reside in the *laini*.

The idea of *laini* ('lines') was a radical departure from the older and common settlement pattern in Siaya. These 'new' men and women were consciously attempting to make the Liganua Church rather than the clan their social focus. The Church became the centre of a new social life. One historian, Florida Karani, has noted that:

'At the Church-Villages, the founders and elders assumed social responsibilities of their Christian communities. Hence they assumed some of the roles of the clan elder. This put them in a strategic position to influence those who came under them. A stage was set whereby Western influences could filter in without encountering serious challenge or resistance and consequently large sections of the community got unhinged from the traditional set-up and became involved in a new way of life.'[3]

The new community remained separate from the day-to-day affairs of the older community of Liganua. But as the families developing in the *laini* grew and overran the available lands, life in the *laini* became unmanageable, and occupants moved away to look for more land, typically returning to their lineage lands.

Liganua is a small community in Siaya, 80km from the

substantial town of Kisumu, much farther removed from the distant outposts of Nairobi and Kampala. Yet Liganua, like other neighbourhoods of western Kenya, was the locus of a substantial and critical expansion of thought and activity. One hundred years ago, the people of Liganua moved their cattle back and forth along, and across, the Rabolo. They were preoccupied, perhaps, with the quality of their pastures (*lek*) and their grains.

By the mid-twentieth century, their horizons had widened enormously, and they now spoke of Kampala, Kisumu, and Mombasa, whether they had travelled there or not. They discussed the funeral arrangements of the *mzungu*, and played at tennis on the paths of the village. The responses to new vistas brought about by the colonial situation, and specifically introduced to the life and conversation of Liganua by *jopango* and *josomo*, were so varied as to defy simple generalizations. The material goods of the people of Liganua were augmented by *kibrit* (matches), *chumbi* (salt), and *chai* (tea). The very language of authority was elaborated: *disi* (DC), *waskar* (askari), *polis* (police), and *jaj* (judge) became familiar and common usages. The vocabulary of subjection seeped into Liganua as well: *jangli* (bushman), *swaini* (swine), *kafiri* (kaffir), *bladi fuul* (bloody fool), were used in stories of oppressive work elsewhere and came to be used in everyday discourse among Liganua folk. Ideas about *us* and *them* were enriched with enhanced knowledge about the others.

The *Joleplep*: the 'fast-movers'

Urban dwellers often cull their small talk from radio and newspaper reports, thus resonating what the ruling classes consider to be 'news'. In Siaya, the villagers have their own perspective as to what constitutes news, and often produce and circulate their own news quite independently of the established public and official reports. At Boro, the passing of the district commissioner's Land Rover may elicit only fleeting comment: maybe it has been repainted, or he has a new driver. District officers may or may not be known, or identifiable. The people who may most often engage the minds of Boro men and women are their own fringe elements rather than those from outside: the appearance in the market of the madmen Ojow and Nyasio; the odd-jobs men who seem to be incapable of doing anything which does not defy authority, from being electioneering agents for James Orengo (who stood against Minister Matthews Ogutu in the 1980 parliamentary elections), to being abductors of reluctant brides for men of the Nairobi salariat who have not the time to haggle through endless bridewealth negotiations. These men, Okach

Ogada, Agunga Charlie, and Otumba Apiyo, among them, provided in the 1970s and early 1980s an alternative society for the
people of Siaya to talk about. Order, in their minds, in their
public expression, was fine if it suited their intentions; but there
were always other ways of going about things. They became
known as *joleplep* (the 'fast-movers') and provided material for
local talk about authority, about society, in the turbulent political
and economic Siaya landscape of the 1970s.

The Christmas disco

In December 1979, several young people arranged for a permit
to hold a disco dance in Boro around the Christmas holiday.
On the appointed evening, several hundred young people
assembled. Each young man paid a shilling and a half and each
young woman paid fifty cents. Given the conditions, a good
sound system and a good selection of Western rock, Kenya,
Zaïre, and reggae discs, the affair generated a collective
exuberance unlike anything that the young of Boro had organized
before. After a hour or so, the two Boro policemen arrived. Having apparently already enjoyed themselves drinking away the
early evening, they told the organizers they were going to oversee
the dance. The organizers insisted that, as their permit was in
good order, and the dance was going smoothly, their official
presence was not required and that if the policemen wanted to
pay the entrance fee they could join the dancers. The policemen
retired to one of the bars on the market square and, after a couple more drinks, returned to the dance. This time they announced
that the dance was a 'public nuisance' and that they were going
to 'close it down instantly'. There was a gigantic uproar and
several of the dancers charged at the police, knocking them to
the ground and kicking them. The police ran off in the direction of the administrative offices. The dance continued without
further trouble and at the given hour the young of Boro
disbanded and went their way, the organizers clearing up the
ground and securing their record player and speakers.

The next day, Christmas Eve, found the two policemen scour-
ing the Boro market place for some of the young people who
had chased them off the night before. They found one young
boy and started beating him. A small crowd formed, mostly composed of young people, jeering the policemen for what they were
doing. According to one witness:

'Several in the crowd suddenly jumped forward, pulled away
the young boy, and started beating the policemen. One of the
policemen was knocked to the ground with a piece of fencing
and was getting hit pretty badly. His colleague picked him up
and dragged him away toward the administrative offices. A *117*

quarter of an hour later, a government Land Rover appeared, driven by one of the policemen, with the other in the back, and with a woman in the passenger's seat. She was the acting assistant district officer, sent from far away to handle the administrative offices in Boro while the ADO was on long leave near Nairobi. The Land Rover charged the now larger crowd of young people near the market. People threw everything they could find at the Land Rover as it backed, turned, and charged again and again. Someone with a large steel pole smashed the windscreen, and the two policemen and the woman started to get the worst of it. The Land Rover was stopped and now the crowd got around to one side and tried to turn the vehicle over. Elijah Oduor, chief assistant in the archaeological camp, rushed down the road from a spot near the camp and yelled into the crowd to let the acting ADO go. The crowd held off, and then backed off, and the Land Rover started up and turned and headed toward Siaya, where there was a large administrative police force. The crowd scattered in every direction. They expected an onslaught of a hundred police within the hour.'

Elijah returned to the archaeological camp across the road from the Boro police post and administrative offices and went back to work, but also kept a watch on the Boro—Siaya road. That day, no officials or police came from Siaya. The next day, Christmas Day, again there was no evidence of police activity along the Siaya road. Little knots of young people began to meet to evaluate the situation. No evidence of Siaya's authority the next day, either, or the following day. On 30 December the cook at the ADO's station returned from short leave, entirely in the dark about what had happened, yet aware that the various administrative offices were abandoned, and not entirely locked. On 31 December the cook began to refer inquiries to Elijah at the camp across the road. A few people from the neighbourhood of Boro stopped by to see whether Elijah thought the cattle market would open. Elijah remarked that if the ADO were there, the cattle market would be declared closed because of health problems, so they acted as if the order had been given. Market days came and went in normal fashion as if nothing had happened. The teachers opened the schools and began their classes as scheduled. The magistrate had gone to a course in Nairobi and his court was not expected to be opened for several weeks. The only variations from surface normality were that there were no policemen in Boro and the ADO's office was shut.

On 7 January the ADO returned from leave, and Elijah and others in the camp went across the road to greet him after his long absence. He promised assistance to the historical and archaeological research in Boro, but nothing was said about the acting ADO, the two policemen, or the 'Christmas disco'. A few days later, two new policemen arrived at the Boro station in a repaired Land Rover, and still nothing was said. Soon, gossip was around that the Acting ADO had gone to Kisumu, then straight home, and had later returned to Kisumu for a new assignment, that the two policemen had been rebuked for abandoning their posts and transferred to another division. There had been, and there were to be, no arrests, punishment, retribution, or inquiry; indeed, there was no formal word at all.

None of the young people in Boro knew which outsiders had knowledge of the events surrounding their 'Christmas disco', and some who talked about the events realized that they might have to live for a while with the anxiety of not knowing whether their 'revolution' was unknown outside the neighbourhood of Boro or whether the silence from beyond in fact betrayed a strategy of response by the authorities. But they did know that without any sort of formal organization, and without any specific leadership, and only through the context of a rare moment of collective activity and exuberance, they had acted to correct what they had seen as a terrible abuse of police authority.

'A man is a man . . .'

The signature tune from the Luo broadcasting service of the Voice of Kenya runs:

Ng'ato to en ng'ato
Ma kata ineno ni ochalo nadi
Dhano to en dhano
Ka ma noyikee ni mana tie.

(A person is a person
However mean he looks
His Being is Being
He will always have a place
Wherein to be buried.)

One of the more striking features of Siaya is the extent to which economic differentiation can generate distinctions between people of the same age cohort. A man of Siaya may be living in a palace by the Ahero wayside while his childhood friend may have to eke out a living as a paddy-rice grower on a two-hectare mud plot nearby. Some rural people have sought to mediate some of the tension that has emerged because of this differentiation by reiterating the essential humanity of all beings; the sense of this is presented in the Voice of Kenya song. Malele Olunya, an acute observer of the Ndere-Liganua scene, having decided for himself that all labour is drudgery, refuses to work for anyone, and he continually reminds the employers of wage-labour in his neighbourhood not to be haughty, arrogant, and distant from those they employ. Malele does recognize the fact that there is differentiation between *tajiri*, the rich, and *raia*, the ordinary people; indeed, he comments on it frequently, but he is known for his most familiar refrain, 'ng'ato to en ng'ato', 'a man is a man for all that'. It is a refrain that reaches out for moral equity in circumstances where economic equity is not to be dreamt of.[4]

'His head rings books'

One of the skills sought by younger Luo is the ability to introduce new knowledge or new frameworks into day-to-day discourse. It is assumed that one does not burst into the known framework, into the familiar structures, with a mass of new knowledge that may disrupt the known social order. Knowledge is managed, delivered in small doses. It intrudes gently, like a suggestion, like an aside, but should not shock. The deliverer must prepare the recipient. There is an etiquette about how to deliver a message, especially about bereavement. There are ground rules and various common sayings; songs and expressions taunt and suppress the rush-hour mentality where it raises it head. An example of such a saying is,

> In ichop
> Gi ma kolwer
> In iwuoth
> Gi law teke
> Iluoro Lwar.

> (You will burst in
> With the unpruned.
> You may wrap yourself with a raw cowhide.
> You anticipate
> Grey hairs.)

Behind the veneer of harmony, or in competition with the ideal of harmony, is the recognition that there is rivalry and competition between individuals, or societies. The essence of this dialectical competition is captured by this rendition of Apuot (in his praise song for Adongo):

> *Solo*: Ng'ato loso
> To ng'ato ketho
> *All*: Enying Adongo
> Ka Rajula

> *Solo*: Ng'ato sero
> To ng'ato semo
> *All*: Enying Adongo

Ka Rajula

Solo: Ng'ato Ong'eyo
To ng'ato kia
All: Adongo
Wod Nyamin Ondoro

Solo: Polo K'larie Ndalo.

(The one builds
The other destroys
That's his name
Adongo son of Rajula

The one woos
The other dissuades
That's his name
Adongo son of Rajula.

One knows
The other doesn't know
Adongo
Son of Ondoro's sister.

There are no land disputes
In heaven.)

The two lives of Hajiga, a 'villain' on Majimbo Island, indicate a consciousness concerning oppositions and options. His song 'Night-time' runs,

Odiechieng;
To wan Ji

Otieno
to wan Le.

(Daytime
We are Humans

Night-time
We are Animals.)

There is in Kenya the image of a 'Luo man' as an educated person, with powerful intellectual skills, and a commanding arrogance. The image disguises remarkable facts: for example almost 50 per cent of the school-age children in Siaya did not attend schools regularly in 1985 and public examination results of students in and from Siaya proceed on what is broadly described as 'their abysmal course'. The Siaya community does

121

not present itself to the outsider as stridently or obsessively involved with schooling. Throughout the colonial period there were few schools in Siaya, and schooling as a crucible of cultural values sparred uneasily with other value systems. There was no triumph of the idea of 'school' as the crux of a community's present and future such as emerged early in the colonial era in many parts of Africa.

In Siaya a dialectic appeared, and was positionally stable, between the *josomo*, the 'schooled' and the *jopiny* or *jokoyo*, the 'untainted Luo'. A song of the 1930s captures the tension between these two elements:

> Josomo obuogo Jokoyo
> Gi Wa-gi-e We
> Jokoyo obuogo Josomo
> Gi law Nyadiel.

> (Josomo frighten Jokoyo
> With Wa-and-e = We
> Jokoyo frighten Josomo
> With a goatskin loincloth.)

Indeed, it is important to note that the idea of education, of schooling, as a 'taint' survived powerfully in Siaya right through the colonial period.

Each side was deemed potent in this sparring match. In Siaya, the *jonanga*, the man perceived to be 'Westernizing', was visibly competing with the proper Luo man of culture *jamaranda*, well into the 1950s. It is in this context that those who received Western education are seen by people of Siaya today to stand out so boldly, so much in contrast to their age-mates: Ezekiel Apindi, Paul Mbuya, John Paul Olola, and Simeon Nyende in the 1920s and 1930s; Oginga Odinga, Omuodo Ayila and Joel Meshack Ojal in the 1940s; Argwings Kodhek in the 1950s; and Simeon Ominde, David Wasawo, and Bethwell Allan Ogot in the 1960s. These were *josomo*, and were the heroes of the bookmen, but they were not the only heroes in the Siaya landscape. These schooled men were, in the 1960s and 1970s, gradually integrated, redomesticated, into the language idiom of the nineteenth century. They were now to be seen as *jorieko*, clever people, with their pedigree derived, explainable, from the Luo magicians, diviners, and medicinemen of the early twentieth century: Obondo Mumbo and Gor Mahia had been their progenitors. The internal contradictions within Christianity did not escape the observation of the *jokoyo*, even as these thought-to-be 'Westernizers' claimed to be different, shunning the ways of the Luo world. Catholics, people noted, drank beer after all. This called for comment, in a song:

> Din Kopere
> Din mimadhoe kong'o
> Din gi Duado won Omondi
> Din mimadhoe kong'o.

> (Opere's Dini.
> They consume beer
> Duado Omondi's Dini
> Consumes beer.)

Important contrasts are insinuated within this song. Here is a case of intentional ambiguity, of a society deliberately processing the incoming product at its own pace, in its own time, in its own language. A holder of a PhD degree is referred to in Siaya as *ajuoga*, diviner or witchdoctor, with all the ambiguities that the term has held for these communities during the last millennium.

One of the intriguing aspects of the discourse about education among those who might be called the Luo middle classes is this multiplicity of voices. Conventional wisdom among this coterie has it that 'the Luo are educated, and they love education'. Yet from among the ranks of this same stratum the sentiment *somo ok gimoro* — 'education is nothing' — is often heard. It is sometimes a conscious reflection of how many educated people have failed to acquire material wealth and, conversely, how many have come from the bottom of the class list and have made wealth in real life. It can also be an indication of well-articulated complexes. One may say: 'I may not be as educated as you but dollar-for-dollar you can't match me, Jack', an utterance attributed to J., and well known among the elite and middle-aged Nairobi Luo. Yet, since the 1940s, even as some demean and mock schooling, education and the educated have continued to be valorized. Those who have acquired education are praised, as in the song by a guitarist of the late 1940s, Oyugi Tobi:

> Opondo Omin Arianda
> Ngat ma nene Osomo
> Ma buk Ochot e wiye.

> (Opondo, the brother of Arianda
> One who reads
> Until his head
> Rings books.)

In the early 1950s, Argwings Kodhek captured the minds of his age-mates in Kenya by graduating simultaneously in sociology and law from the University College of Aberystwyth and London University respectively, having completed the whole project of higher education in the United Kingdom in a space of three years. Myths emerged among the villagers of Gem and Alego about this feat. The school-age neophytes in Liganua were encouraged by Simeon Othieno Odiemo to learn hard, go to Makerere and to England, and to be like Argwings, 'who was so clever that the Queen gave him two degrees and a white wife as a present'. Likewise, David Wasawo, the first Luo PhD, was reputed to be 'so diligent that he skinned an earthworm and dried its hide'.

Such was the ultimate mark of cleverness in the late 1950s. And yet, behind the granaries, the villagers could at the same time afford to giggle about all this cleverness. Otumba Apiyo tells of the story of a villager in Sakwa Kapiyo who was clearly disappointed by the misdirection of a son's development: 'We sent Omamo to India to learn medicine and surgery so as to be useful to the country. But what skill does the man return home with? How to cut cabbages!' Clearly, the villager had his own ranking of the village's needs, and agriculture, which Omamo had read, was a low priority compared to medicine.

Even as the pantheon of Luo intellectual heroes expanded in the late 1950s with the return of the first graduates, including Nicholas Otieno Thombo 'Thrombosis', Bethwell Allan Ogot, and Simeon Hongo Ominde, a core institutional ideology was evolved. Maseno, the pioneer high school in Nyanza, became a shrine for its ardent old boys, with Calleb Yaya, Wilson Ndolo Ayah, and Opondo Mangal Singh weaving a theology about it through the rhetorical question: 'I never saw you at Maseno; how can you be learned?' What had started as chance, with the headmen forcing orphans and poor neighbour's children into Maseno School in 1906, had by the 1960s become a credo to be held onto amidst the turbulence of uncertain careers and rival institutional networks within the wider canvas of Kenya society.

In the shadows

'Wat imedo gi osiep' ('friendship fortifies kinship'), say people of Siaya, as if to challenge mainstream anthropological literature, which has tended to treat kinship as an enclosed, autonomous, locus of structure. Siaya oratory, and the evocations of the Siaya landscape, posit an anthropology, one which serves up examples of kinship as the dynamic crucible of construction of the society, but also which challenges the encompassing force and meaning of kinship in the society. The 'oral traditions', the stories told, are replete with the repetitive stories of fissure at the centre of society, between brother and brother, canonized in the ubiquitous lost-spear and lost-bead story. Indeed, Siaya town is built on the site of one such lost-bead ground, Bar Nyathi, the place of the child's sacrifice.

As if conjuring evidence for the student determined to demonstrate the encompassing logic of kinship, stories told every-day are replete with *nyiego*, the deadly rivalry between co-wives. Twentieth-century lore, even of today, is full of *juok*, the engage-ment of witchcraft by brother against brother. There are the memories of tidy and enclosed kinship groups of the *gunda bur* or *dala*, with kinship, *wat*, as the entire organizing principle of the world — simultaneously a juncture with the comparative tradition in structural-functional anthropology.[5] Is or is not 'the western Kenya Luo' a situation comparable to the Nuer with organization by the 'segmentary lineage principle'? Is this continuous representation of values of kinship a way of critically examining a perceived world in which the absent kin, now dis-tant wage labourers, leave gaps in the work groups and collec-tivities of affection in the countryside?

There are other histories known, and sometimes told, in Siaya that are less clearly supportive of the models that anthropologists have produced to 'cover' Siaya. They are, perhaps, exceptions to 'rules', but they force the observer of Siaya to ask whether new ways of comprehending Siaya might be appropriate, not simply because the invokers of the 'segmentary lineage model' may have erred in its application to western Kenya, nor because the society might be changing in its nature away from an older or 'traditional pattern', nor because the purposes of originally invoking the 'segmentary' model are uniquely registered in the history of the discipline of anthropology.

Rather, such new ways of comprehending Siaya might be appropriate because the referencing of matter through the intellectual exchange of an externally derived sociological model may miss the vital ways in which people in Siaya are and have been attempting to make sense of their past and their histories, not only the public oratories about important migrations but also the darker histories of quiet personal discourse. One speaks in quiet tones about the uncle who has abandoned those children he is responsible for by migrating singly to South Nyanza, creating several orphans in an afternoon. One hears the sub-dued discussion concerning a woman deploying *sihoho*, spells, against the children of co-wives. There are whispers about several brothers in Gem hiring a murder squad to liquidate a whole family because of a land dispute.

At one level, the clan, the lineage, kinship, is constantly invoked, when it comes to the collections of contributions for school fees, funerals, and court-fines. *Wat*, kinship, is voiced by migrant labourers seeking accomodation and initial financial support in towns. At one glance, kinship is the key principle for the observer. But at another glance, *osiepe* (friendship) achieves heightened importance for the observer. 'Families have dangers', 'they never stop coming after me for money', 'I went for help and came away empty' are commonly enough voiced and heard messages that contain, within an alternative anthropology, an anthropology of the shadows, in which the value of loyalty to a friend, *osiep*, is given a critical centrality; and in which there is danger and disappointment associated with family, with kin.

One can return to the *gunda bur* and observe the vital alliances among non-kin that made possible the taking and holding of fortified settlements in the early settled zones of Nyanza; one can hear *pim* in the *siwindhe* bringing intelligence of a wider world into the *dala*, in which the lives and experiences of non-kin are made accessible to the young of the *siwindhe*.

It is perhaps simplistic to offer the suggestion that we are observing two social networks — kinship and friendship — in tension with one another. The 'demography of night-time' is illuminating in this regard. Kambesi, aged 20, goes to Nairobi to find 'decent work', to 'earn some money to get a wife', to 'help his mother with the other children'. Kambesi immediately visits several of his kin in Nairobi; he stays the first night with a brother, the second night with an uncle. He writes home to his mother that he is well and that family are helping him. But in staying with the brother, or the uncle, he is also staying not with kin, for the brother and uncle do not reside alone, but reside with mates whom they have fallen in among in Nairobi. The brother's place is not a good location for looking for work, it requires a good deal of transport money; indeed, many nights, reports the brother, he sleeps elsewhere. The uncle's place is all right, but food is short. Sometimes the uncle travels off to friends to get a meal and spends the night there. One day Kambesi goes with the uncle to one of these friends and spends the night; another day he finds himself travelling with the brother. He meets other people who offer him a corner of a room for a night. Kambesi has become part of a shifting population; a complex 'demography of night-time' that escapes, outruns, the observations of any daylight census-taker and mother's confidence that her son is staying with family. For Kambesi, as for those in the ancient *gunda bur*, 'Wat imedo gi osiep' ('friendship fortifies kinship'); indeed, it may supplant *wat* (kinship) in terms of Kambesi's everyday life, while interested observers might find comfort that 'Kambesi is staying with his uncles in Nairobi'. A working system of affective relations lies in the shadows of a pervasive ideology of kinship, yet for some, and at times, *osiepe* (friendship) begins to gather value, meaning, and construct ideology.

The constitution of an *osiepe* ideology in the twentieth century, perhaps in very recent decades, has an urban context. In the *gweng*, the countryside settlement, one could, eighty or one hundred years ago, operationalize both *wat* (kinship) and *mbas* (age-mates), comrades not kin, as a meaningful coterie of mutual support. With the continuous process of labour migration, there are new challenges for the collectivity of kin: the 12,000 shillings required to move the corpse of a railway labourer from Makongeni Nairobi to Seme Kolunje; the 40,000 shilling deposit required to be paid to the Ministry of Education to enable a young Kanyamwa kinsman to travel to India for higher education; the perennial lawyers' fees to be paid for kinsmen who are perennially engaged in both white-collar and petty theft at their places of work. Even the better-off relations, and even those who constantly invoke the values of kinship, resist siphoning off their savings into what they consider 'these endless tunnels'.

It is here that friendship has moved toward a centrality, and has gathered special meaning, for the urban person. Friends help the Siaya woman or man cope with stresses in town. They are perceived as being ready to make sacrifices for their friends. In public discourse about *wat* and *osiepe*, the friend is deemed to be more selfless. Interaction with friends demands no reciprocity, involves no contracting for future compensation; a failure to contribute does not sever the community; and contributions and empty pockets are not engraved in the memory forever. The tension between two casts of support may have long been present, but the particular social and economic stresses of the city, along with its complex demographies, have stirred the composition of a discourse about support — and perhaps an ideology of friendship — that itself fortifies the older wisdom of Gangu that 'Wat imedo gi osiep'.

NOTES

1. This discussion of Liganua is drawn from E. S. Atieno Odhiambo, 'The movement of ideas: a case study of intellectual responses to colonialism among the Liganua peasants', in B. A. Ogot (ed.), *History and Social Change*

in East Africa (Nairobi, East African Literature Bureau, 1976), pp. 165-85.

2. See Margaret Jean Hay, 'Economic change in Luoland: Kowe, 1890-1945', PhD dissertation, University of Wisconsin, Madison, 1972, pp. 170-4, for an excellent discussion of this distinction between target and career migrants: 'The evidence . . . casts doubt on the widely held assumption that all of the labor migrants during this period were "target workers" . . . More than half of the labor migrants who first left Kowe before 1930 stayed away for periods of fifteen to twenty years. They were certainly not "target workers", and in fact, came close to becoming permanent migrants.' (p. 172) For a reiteration of this argument, see Gavin Kitching, *Class and Economic Change in Kenya: The Making of an African Petite-Bourgeoisie* (New Haven, Yale University Press, 1980), pp. 48-50.

3. Florida Karani 'The history of Maseno School, 1906-1962, its alumni and the local society', MA thesis, University of Nairobi, March 1974, p. 257. For an extended treatment of local religious and political leadership in the colonial period, see John M. Lonsdale, 'A political history of Nyanza, 1883-1945', PhD dissertation, Cambridge University, 1964.

4. David A. Goldenberg has, for a Luo community in South Nyanza, produced an important study of the ways in which observed and operative social and economic differentiation is mediated and suppressed. See his, 'We are all brothers: the suppression of consciousness of socio-economic differentiation in a Kenya Luo lineage', PhD dissertation, Brown University, 1982.

5. A fine, sensitive, and early anthropological study of kinship and lineage formation is Aidan Southall, *Lineage Formation Among the Luo* (London, Oxford University Press, 1952).

Conclusion

Siaya is a consummate labour reserve, with its rural population dependent on the remittances of distant wage labourers and its urban population dependent on the reserve resources — social, cultural, and material — of the countryside. The experience of labour migration and the related transformation of the countryside cuts deep. They leave their artifacts: the early blanket of Atieno Oyugi, Wilson Oluoch Oton's tennis racquet, the empty *kikapu*, the *gorogoro* in its diminishing sizes, the sack of maize, the 'tired soil', the cast-off clothing of Boro market, the unprofitable farm in the sugar belt, and the butcheries . . . in one sense just a few things sliding off the edge of a periphery of the world economy.

Yet Siaya is also a landscape or landscapes moulded by people in real time. Not only is the *gunda bur* — by considerable collective effort — scooped out of the earth as a form of concentrated settlement some centuries ago, but it is also invested with meaning by those in Siaya in this century who reflect back upon the transformations that have shaped their present world. The juxtaposition of the remains of these ancient settlements and present patterns of land occupation and use stimulate Luo of Siaya to 'read' the physical world and understand for themselves the nature of change in their realm. In this, knowledge is critical, and knowledge dissolves and supplants a notion of an overarching power of custom. The figure *pim* is recalled as a woman who brought intelligence of other people and places into the household and utilized it in the nurturing and socialization of children. Individuals like Ogola brought home for Christmas stories of Uganda, critical information and playful accounts alike. By 1910 people of Liganua were learning about the Norfolk Hotel from James Lucas Oganga, who was employed there, while Okoth Ka Opiyo brought back to Siaya information about the agricultural estates of Lord Delamere, where he was working as a herdboy. The *jopith* and the *josemb dhok* gathered and utilized *129* secret knowledge of market conditions and police and veterinary interventions in extending and operating their cattle enterprises. Othieno Odiemo is remembered in Liganua for what he had learned about the variable meanings of beauty of women at the Coast. Ayany and Malo gathered information and produced distinctive histories of the Luo of Kenya. Young people in the countryside reflect upon the sexual conduct of their urban peers, as their urban counterparts reciprocally reflect upon the country practice.

This knowledge is not simply 'about knowing', about having good stories to tell over a beer pot or good stories to tell the next researcher. It is significantly about authority, about the ways in which understandings of the forms and locations of power and of control and domination were evolved, gathered, sifted, revised, and given life within the conversations and arguments of Luo.

Occasionally, the Luo of Kenya, with other Kenyans, participate in large national debates surrounding, for example, the dissolution of the Kenya Peoples' Union (KPU), Tom Mboya's death, the Kenyatta succession, or the present interests of Oginga Odinga. At a different level, Siaya voters discharge their parliamentary representatives with impunity in the general elections. There is hardly a word about these matters in this present work. Some may suggest that there is, in the end, actually little *political* in the representation of Siaya offered here. Indeed, little is presented about local administration in the colonial period and independence. The national party hardly appears at all. The state appears only intermittently, though when it does it does so powerfully, in such discussions as maize policy and veterinary and price control in the cattle and meat business. Kenyatta and Odinga, two giant statesmen of post-colonial Kenya, appear in this work as authors to be read and cited rather than as officials.

Yet the present work is heavily *political* in its orientation in another sense. The warm memories of *pim* are understood not only as sources on earlier practices of nurturing and socialization but as stern critiques of the present nature of family and of schooling. The Christmas Disco episode suggests the incredible power produced of ambiguity in its unclosed 'conclusion'. The comparisons of 'Kenya' and 'Uganda' that returning Luo brought back to their homes in the colonial period provided material for the construction of powerful and enduring concepts of work and opportunity. The work of Ayany and Malo in moulding histories of the Luo past was work of subliminal contest over the question of primacy among different forms of association, and of the legitimacy and dominance of specific coteries in western Kenya. The references to football are simultaneously references to the solidarity of Luo people within the Kenyan polity and of the capacity of a dispersed population to organize itself for action within a nation-state. The manifold pressures and appeals placed upon women and men to strengthen their associations with their countryside homes, involving investments, reorganization of time, and reworking of household management, are again political. Food is, pre-eminently, about power; and discussions among the folk of Siaya about scarcity, about the quality of soil, about diet and taste and food colour, about the *gorogoro*, about prices, and about women's control of household economies, are in a very fundamental sense about the distribution of power and rights in the wider society. The amusing gambits of the *jogam* are, at their heart, about the control of the person and body of Adhiambo and of her child, in a struggle among the groom, Adhiambo's family, and Adhiambo herself. The stories of accumulation, of the wealth in the sugar belt, and of the songs and slogans that soften and mediate observed social or economic differentiation among Siaya folk, are intensely political, both in their inward parody and self-critique, and in dealing with the tension surrounding the possibility of ethnic and political solidarity across class lines.

It would be a mistake to perceive this 'political commotion' as simply or principally reactive to, or directed at, the *state* or at some notional wider world economy. The wider economy certainly does constitute the labour reserve in the countryside, yet our observations suggest a far deeper and denser process, one that is local, personal, and very often intimate in its motors and in its expression. Satisfactions and meanings are sought by Siaya folk that involve the handling and comprehension of materials from many arenas, and from the past. The analyses and representations concerning the past, the Luo, and the state, and concerning change, opportunity, and scarcity, are real and powerful in and of themselves. And they outrun the capacities of historians and other humanists and social scientists (including the present authors) to encapsulate them in academic tomes. The power of these analyses and representations perhaps lies in that they are evolved from, and are expressed toward, the 'anthropology of the shadows'.

This deeper political terrain is one of unresolved mediations of variable interests and conflicting notions of reality and custom. If there is power in custom in Siaya, it is in the way in which debates over the authenticity and purpose of custom expose custom as an aspect of authority. If there is a cultural basis in custom it is not in a list of Luo traits observable in Siaya, but rather in the way in which certain idioms are carried between *131* social fields, as in the boat launching as a marriage, or in the use of segmentary lineage metaphors in discussions of the history of Kenya's football clubs. What is often most critical in these discussions, and what is most likely to be missed, is that such discourses within Siaya work upon the little and often intimate solidarities and oppositions among kin and comrades that give form and direction to Luo culture and society. If broader and larger forces define the material and political position of the reserve, Elijah, Nashon, and their friends are constructing myriad pathways to the formation of ideas concerning the locations, uses, meanings, and moral values of authority. Perhaps we should ask to what extent is it in the calculus of this everyday behaviour of helping a friend, seeking a romance, organizing a dance, scrounging in a market place, participating in a rally, hanging out, caring for one's physical person, that the architecture of social and political life gathers its form and is carried into new moments and other places?

Thu Tinda!

Afterword:
Silvanus Melea Otieno

In the late seventeenth or early eighteenth century a group of Luo speakers arrived in south-central Busoga in Uganda. In the twentieth century, this group is recalled as having established in this area the small Bugweri kingdom. The leader of the group is remembered by the name of *Kakaire*. Kakaire is held to have been the founder of the Bugweri dynasty two and a half centuries ago. Between 1919 and 1938, Y.K. Lubogo, a translator, clerk, and chief in the local administrative service of Busoga, collected material on the histories of the various and numerous Busoga states and assembled them into *A History of Busoga* finally published only in an English translation in 1960. Lubogo provided an account of Kakaire's death and burial:

'One day Kakaire decided to go to Wangobo and improve his *mbuga* [capital, enclosure] there. As soon as he arrived he fell seriously ill and died suddenly. His people decided to bury him there in honour of his first home. They made a very deep grave for his body, which they wrapped in wonderful bark-cloth, and then gently lowered it into the deep tomb. They left the grave uncovered until they could get all the things necessary for the burial ceremonies from Bunyoro [where he was purportedly born, hundreds of miles to the west]. Three days passed and the grave was still uncovered. On the fourth day, as the people were crowded along the edge of the grave, lamenting and wailing for their dead master, the sky suddenly darkened with thick black clouds; strong winds blew, making trees squeak mournfully, and great clouds of dust flew up into the air, blinding the people, who could hear nothing. At last the storm calmed down and the people were able to look around. To their dismay and great astonishment, they saw nothing of the dead body — it had disappeared during the storm. This discovery not only bewildered them more but also increased their bereavement. After eight days a large stone was found properly laid in the grave in place of the body which had disappeared. This stone can still be seen

133

as a large rock. The amazing disappearance of the body affected the people of Bugweri so much that they decided against burying any of their dead chiefs at Wangobo.'[1]

In early 1987, the High Court of Kenya removed itself to Westlands Cottage Hospital, Nairobi, for the purpose of taking testimony from an elderly gravedigger and mason from Siaya District, Mr Albert Ong'ang'o, who lay in the hospital following surgery. Under careful examination by two barristers, Richard Otieno Kwach and John Khaminwa, Mr Ong'ang'o recalled a day a few years earlier when he was digging a grave at Nyamila (Nyamira), Siaya District, for Mr Simon (or Simeon) Odhiambo, who had fallen sick and died in Nairobi Hospital. He described to the court how, as he was standing in the grave with his assistants, the recently departed's brother, Mr S.M. Otieno, the distinguished Nairobi criminal lawyer, had stooped down over the edge of the grave. Ong'ang'o recalled that as S.M. Otieno had leaned over the hole he had called down to him, 'Albert, Albert, you have prepared my brother's grave. In case I die, you will also prepare mine next to my father's.'[2]

In early 1987, the Nairobi advocate Timan Njugi presented himself as a witness before the same High Court proceeding. Mr Njugi recalled how, as counsel to the Miller Commission of Inquiry into the conduct of former Attorney General of Kenya Charles Njonjo, he had worked closely with S.M. Otieno, who was serving as a consultant to the Commission. Njugi recalled how, one day in early 1984, he and several others were seated in a Nairobi office awaiting Mr Otieno's arrival. S.M. Otieno entered the office, greeted his friends, and, according to Njugi, announced, 'Mussajjah, I've bought a piece of land in Kiserian (Ngong) [a short distance to the west of Nairobi] . . . I shall be buried at Kiserian and I have made this plainly clear to all parties that might be interested in my funeral. I shall be buried at Kiserian.'[3]

* * *

S.M. Otieno (aged 55) died at 6.00 p.m., Saturday, 20 December 1986 in Nairobi Hospital, after falling sick earlier in the day. On 28 December, the *Daily Nation* of Nairobi reported that:
'Mrs Wambui Otieno and Mr. Joash Ochieng Ougo announce over the Voice of Kenya conflicting burial places for the late lawyer. She says that her late husband will be buried at their Upper Matasia farm, Ngong, on Saturday, January 3, 1987, while Mr Ochieng's announcement says the burial will take place the same day but at Nyamila Village, Nyalgunga Sub-location, Alego Central, Siaya District.'[4]

The following day the *Daily Nation* reported further conflict over the plans for removing Otieno's body from the City Mortuary for a public viewing, and for the burial arrangements. The paper announced that funeral announcements in regard to Otieno's burial had been halted by the Voice of Kenya.

In the days which followed, court orders and injunctions blocked the plans of the widow and the brother for ceremonies on 3 January 1987. Whereas in testimony eventually given before the High Court of Kenya, the widow had declared that her husband had announced, in her presence, that 'If I died and you pass Westlands (in Nairobi) on the way to Nyamila, I will kick the coffin open, come out and beat up all those in the convoy and go back into my coffin',[5] S.M. Otieno was finally buried not at his Ngong farm but rather at Nyamila village, Nyalgunga, in Siaya District, on 23 May 1987, more than five months after his death.

S.M. Otieno's two declarations — reported by the two witnesses under oath before the High Court — framed an immense and complex 154 day legal struggle over the disposition of his body, concluded only by a final judgement handed down by the Court of Appeal, Kenya's highest court. The contest for control of his remains pitted his widow, Virginia Wambui Waiyaki Otieno, a 'Kikuyu lady' and sister of Dr Munyua Waiyaki (a former Minister of Foreign Affairs), against Joash Ochieng Ougo, brother of S.M. Otieno, and Omolo Siranga, head of the Umira Kager clan which claimed S.M. Otieno as one of their own.

In his opening remarks to the High Court, Mr John Khaminwa, representing the widow, set out his view of the case. The issues were, in brief,

'Who in law is entitled to bury the remains of the late S.M. Otieno? What law should apply in this case? This case involves one whom we all knew — S.M. Otieno. The remains of his body are still at the City Mortuary where it has been for the last month and more. The dispute is between his widow Virginia Wambui Otieno and her brother-in-law Joash Ougo Ochieng and Mr Omolo Siranga of the Umira Kager clan and is over who should bury his body. My case is that the widow is, in law, entitled to bury her husband at Upper Matasia. She intends to do so in accordance with S.M. Otieno's wishes. We shall call evidence from Kenyans of all walks of life who will testify it was his wish to be buried in Nairobi or Upper Matasia in Ngong. We shall also demonstrate that the customary law of the Luo community or of any community in Kenya does not arise in this case. We intend to show that the deceased's style of life and his wishes show clearly that it was never his intention to be subject to African customs. I will show by evidence that the late S.M. Otieno spent all his working life in Nairobi, apart from some 16 months when he worked at Kisumu Municipality as deputy town clerk before his return to Nairobi and the opening of his law practice. We all loved and respected Otieno. He was the embodiment of what is best and fine in Kenyan society. It is the desire of his widow to give him a decent Christian burial which is his due. The late S.M. was committed to his wife, family, the rule of law and the Constitution.'[6]

On the fifteenth day of the trial, Richard Kwach, representing the Umira Kager clan and the deceased's brother, offered the case for burial at the clan home in Siaya.

'My lord, I will be submitting that Mr. Otieno's so-called expressed wishes are not consistent with Luo customary law and burial traditions. The main thrust of my case is that there is no written or general law in Kenya which gives the widow the right to claim the body for burial.

. . . My lord, nothing was shown to you to prove Otieno had severed his connections with his ancestral land at Nyalgunga. There was no positive evidence on this. There is no general law on Christian burial in Kenya. This is an area which was deliberately left by Parliament and our forefathers to be governed by the laws of our various tribes. . . . My learned friend said Luo customs relating to burial are discriminatory and unconstitutional. My submission is that they are not. Ever since the world began, all Luo women have not gone to court . . . My lord, in Luoland, certain people do certain things. In burial matters, this is an issue for elders only. My lord, if you are taken to my home, it will not be a question of where you will be buried. But when. There is evidence that all burials are Christian. What is repugnant and immoral in *tero buru* (a ceremony to chase spirits), burning a funeral fire *magenga* or staying out of the house for four days? There is a very good answer to this custom. Women are very migratory in nature. There are certain things that have acquired permanent status. You do not leave burial matters in charge of women.

. . . What . . . [the Judicature Act, Section 2, Sub-section 2] says is that if there is a conflict between written and customary law and one of the parties in the case is affected by customary law, then the customary law applies unless it is repugnant and immoral to justice.

I have searched my mind and cannot come across any burial system that can be said to be repugnant to justice. Everyone, including the plaintiff, accepts that we Luos are not forced to marry anyone after death. Shaving of hair is limited and depends on whether or not one wants to. What harm can you cause with *tero buru*? With the lighting and running of the funeral fire, with the requirement that men have to spend four days beside the *magenga*? My lord, if the evidence was that we Luos cut up our dead, put them in sacks and throw them into the river, then that would be repugnant. We can provide a decent burial just like anyone else. It will be a draconian measure to take away these customs and it is not provided for in law, as my learned friend has requested.

Mrs Otieno went out of her way to marry a Luo and having done that, I submit that she walked out of her tribe and became a Luo. And those are the customs that govern her. This was her final decision. It is an irreversible one. When she got married, she did not acquire any burial rights which anyone wants to remove from her. She found a disciplined order which has been working since time immemorial. She is, I submit, hellbent on creating chaos in the tribe. Mrs Wambui Otieno married a Luo and ceased being a Kikuyu.

. . . the evidence is that Otieno observed customs. He attended funerals at his home, he saw to it that his father was laid to rest properly. He was present when *magenga* was lit and then *tero buru* was performed. There is no evidence that he called in policemen when these things were going on. He slept outside for five nights. My lord, when the huts of Simeon Odhiambo's [S.M.'s brother's] wives were leaking, it is significant that they . . . turned to S.M. Otieno to ask for money to buy the grass to thatch their huts . . . My Lord, I would like to tell you something. When I stand at my home, I can see Otieno's home across the river which separates us. We have been drinking from this river from time immemorial.'[7]

So the case proceeded with counsel presenting ranging argument, bringing forward witnesses to sustain this point and that, countering the witnesses of the opposing side. On the one side, the brother Joash and the Umira Kager clan, with witnesses, sought to affirm, at any legal cost, the primacy for the Luo of the attachment to the homeland, to the location of the 'placenta', of the son to the father, of patrilineage as virtue. On the other side, Mrs Otieno, with numerous witnesses, sought to affirm the indelible status of the 'modern family' in Kenya society, freed from the old practices of a 'dim past', and with it the status that modernity and modern family life gave to women who through circumstances or by choice came to form marriages and constitute households outside the control of clan and tradition. As the sides sought supportive rulings from the courts of the Kenya

137

republic, so they raised up and produced histories and
ethnographies of Luo society which on the one side valorized
and, occasionally, reified tradition and which, on the other,
challenged the worth and validity of traditional practices in what
was argued is a 'modernizing' Kenya society.

As each side's counsel challenged the assertions and witnesses
of the other, the legal contest dragged on into a fifth month, producing an extraordinary debate, or series of debates, over the
force and meaning of 'customary law' and 'customary practice'
in Kenya law, over the power of received English common law
in Kenyan justice, over concepts of death and concepts of property, over the purposes and utilities of burial practices and beliefs
concerning the dead in Kenya, over the relationship between
the 'body' and concepts of material and transferable property
in law, over the status of women in Kenya and the circumstances
of their rights, over the status of Christian belief and practice
in Kenyan social and cultural life, over the concepts of 'home'
(*dala*) and 'residence', over the implications of inter-ethnic marriage in Kenya society, over the nature of the relationship between wife and husband and of the law's capacity to comprehend
the intimate arena of confidence established between a wife and
a husband, and over the meanings and values of 'tradition' and
'modern' in popular Kenyan thought and discourse, and in social
practice.

Many of these debates circle back to the discussions which
the authors of this volume have developed in the text, drafting
virtually the whole volume in the twenty months before S.M.
Otieno died, almost anticipating or rehearsing the lines of argument developed within the case. The point to be made here is
not so much that the authors have achieved some manner of
prediction, but that the debates over what constitutes history,
culture, and society taken up by learned jurists and scholarly
witnesses before the court are thickly replicated and sometimes
powerfully confronted by elaborate discourses within Luo society.

In March, 1987, Elijah Oduor Ogutu, who figures in our text
at various points, wrote to one of the authors of this volume to
report that he had been looking through photographic collections at the National Museums of Kenya for prints which might
be useful in the preparation of our volume. He was 'very much
delayed, however, because I am having difficulties right now
since for several months we have been trying unsuccessfully to
bury our uncle, the lawyer S.M. Otieno.'

Notes

1. (Jinja, East African Literature Bureau, 1960 and 1962), p. 58. Other accounts of this episode relate that the body flew back to Bunyoro (in western Uganda), Kakaire's supposed birthplace.
2. Sean Egan, ed., *S.M. Otieno: Kenya's Unique Burial Saga* (Nairobi, Nation Newspapers, c. 1987), p. 83. This volume presents the case record with a number of additional reports from the *Daily Nation*, Nairobi. Catherine Gicheru and Paul Muhoho are credited as reporters for the entire publication. A useful collection of papers was discussed at a special seminar on the case organized by the Faculty of Law of the University of Nairobi 18 July 1987.
3. Egan, p. 40.
4. *Ibid.*, p. 2.
5. *Ibid.*, p. 22.
6. *Ibid.*, p. 17.
7. *Ibid.*, pp. 94-96.

Bibliography

Amuka, Peter, 'A preliminary discussion of the literary value of two *dodo* songs by Obudo of Homa Bay', UNESCO Seminar on Oral Traditions, Past Growth and Future Development in East Africa, Kisumu, 1979

Ayany, Samuel, *Kar Chakruok Mar Luo* (Kisumu, Equatorial Publishers, 1952)

Ayot, Henry O., *Historical Texts of the Lake Region of East Africa* (Nairobi, Kenya Literature Bureau, 1977)

Ayot, Henry O., *A History of the Luo-Abasuba of Western Kenya from AD 1760-1940* (Nairobi, Kenya Literature Bureau, 1979)

Blount, Ben G., 'Acquisition of language by Luo children', PhD dissertation, University of California, Berkeley, 1969

Blount, Ben G., 'Agreeing to agree on genealogy: a Luo sociology of knowledge', in Mary Sanches and Ben G. Blount (eds), *Sociocultural Dimensions of Language Use* (New York, Academic Press, 1975), pp. 117-35

Blount, Ben G., 'Aspects of Luo socialization', *Language and Society*, 1 (1979)

Blount, Ben G., and Richard T. Curley, 'The southern Luo languages: a glottochronological reconstruction', *Journal of African Languages*, 9, 1 (1970), pp. 1-18

Butterman, Judith M., 'Luo social formations in change: Karachuonyo and Kanyamkago, *c.* 1800-1945', PhD dissertation, Syracuse University, 1979

Buzzard, Shirley, 'Women's status and wage employment in Kisumu, Kenya', PhD dissertation, The American University, 1982

Clifford, James, and George E. Marcus (eds), *Writing Culture: The Poetics and Politics of Ethnography* (Berkeley, University of California Press, 1986)

Cohen, David William, 'The river-lake Nilotes from the fifteenth to the nineteenth century', in B. A. Ogot (ed.), *Zamani: A Survey of East African History, New Edition* (Nairobi, East African

Publishing House and Longman, 1974), pp. 136-49

Cohen, David William, *Womunafu's Bunafu: A Study of Authority in a Nineteenth Century African Community* (Princeton, Princeton University Press, 1977)

Cohen, David William, 'Pim's work: some thoughts on the construction of relations and groups — the Luo of western Kenya', paper presented to a conference on 'The History of the Family in Africa', School of Oriental and African Studies, London, September 1981

Cohen, David William, 'The political transformation of northern Busoga', *Cahiers d'Etudes africaines*, 22, 3-4 (1982), pp. 465-88

Cohen, David William, 'Luo camps in seventeenth century eastern Uganda: the use of migration tradition in the reconstruction of culture', *Sprache und Geschichte in Afrika (SUGIA)*, 5 (1983) pp. 145-75 (a paper originally prepared for and presented to the International Congress of Africanists, Addis Ababa, December, 1973)

Cohen, David William, 'The face of contact: a model of a cultural and linguistic frontier in early eastern Uganda', in Rainer Vossen and Marianne Bechhaus-Gerst (eds), *Nilotic Studies: Proceedings of the International Symposium on Languages and History of the Nilotic Peoples, Cologne, January 4-6, 1982* (Berlin, Dietrich Reimer Verlag, 1983), Vol. 2, pp. 341-55

Cohen, David William, 'Food production and food exchange in the precolonial Lakes Plateau Region', in Robert I. Rotberg (ed.), *Imperialism, Colonialism, and Hunger: East and Central Africa* (Lexington, Mass., Lexington Books, 1983), pp. 1-18

Cohen, David William, 'Christmas discos and other things: the discourse of the dominated in a Kenyan village', paper presented to the 4th International Roundtable in Anthropology and History, Bad Homburg, West Germany, October 1983

Cohen, David William, 'Doing social history from *pim*'s doorway', in Olivier Zunz (ed.), *Reliving the Past: The Worlds of Social History* (Chapel Hill, University of North Carolina Press, 1985)

Cohen, David William, 'Natur und Kampf — Uberfluss und Armut in der Viktoriasee-Region in Afrika von 1880 bis zur Gegenwart', *SOWI*, 14, 1 (1985), pp. 10-23

Crazzolara, J. P., *The Lwoo* (Verona, Editrice Nigrizia, 1950, 1951, and 1954)

DuPré, Carole E., *The Luo of Kenya: An Annotated Bibliography* (Washington, DC, Institute for Cross-Cultural Research, 1968)

Egan, Sean (ed.), *S.M. Otieno: Kenya's Unique Burial Saga* (Nairobi, Nation Newspapers, c. 1987)

Evans-Pritchard, E. E., 'Luo tribes and clans', *Rhodes-Livingstone Journal*, 7 (1949), pp. 24-40

Evans-Pritchard, E. E., 'Ghostly vengeance among the Luo of Kenya', *Man*, 50, 133 (1950), pp. 86-7

Evans-Pritchard, E. E., *The Position of Women in Primitive Societies and Other Essays in Social Anthropology* (New York, The Free Press, 1965)

Fearn, Hugh, *An African Economy: A Study of the Economic Development of Nyanza Province of Kenya, 1903-1953* (London, Oxford University Press, 1956)

Goldenberg, David Asher, 'We are all brothers: the suppression of socio-economic differentiation in a Kenya Luo lineage', PhD dissertation, Brown University, 1982

Hartwig, Gerald, 'The Victoria Nyanza as a trade route in the nineteenth century', *Journal of African History*, 9, 4 (1970), pp. 535-52

Hauge, Hans-Egil, *Luo Religion and Folklore* (Oslo, Scandinavian University Books, 1974)

Hay, Margaret Jean, 'Economic change in Luoland: Kowe, 1890-1945', PhD dissertation, University of Wisconsin, Madison, 1972

Hay, Margaret Jean, 'Local trade and ethnicity in western Kenya', *African Economic History Review*, 2 (1975), pp. 7-12

Hay, Margaret Jean, 'Luo women and economic change during the colonial period', in Nancy J. Hafkin and Edna G. Bay (eds), *Women in Africa: Studies in Social and Economic Change* (Stanford, Stanford University Press, 1976), pp. 87-109

Henige, David, *Oral Historiography* (New York, Longman, 1982)

Herring, Ralph, 'The influence of climate on the migrations of the central and southern Lwo', *Kenya Historical Review*, 4, 1 (1976), pp. 35-62

Herring, Ralph, 'Political development in eastern Africa: the Luo case re-examined', *Kenya Historical Review*, 6, 1-2 (1978), pp. 126-45

Herring, Ralph, 'The JoLuo Before 1900', paper presented to the University of Nairobi History Seminar, 1978

Herring, Ralph, D. W. Cohen, and B. A. Ogot, 'The construction of dominance: the strategies of selected Luo groups in Uganda and Kenya', in Ahmed I. Salim (ed.), *State Formation in Eastern Africa* (Nairobi, Heinemann, 1984), pp. 126-61

Hobley, Charles W., 'Kavirondo', *The Geographical Journal*, 12 (1896), pp. 361-72

Hobley, Charles W., *Kenya: From Chartered Company to Crown Colony* (London, Witnerby, 1929)

Hobsbawn, Eric J. and Terence Ranger, (eds), *The Invention of Tradition* (Cambridge, Cambridge University Press, 1983)

Hutchinson, Dale L., and Clark Spence Larsen, 'Stress and

adaptation at Santa Catalina de Guale: analysis of human remains', paper presented at the Society for Historical Archeology, 9 January 1987

Johnson, Steven L., 'Changing patterns of maize utilization in western Kenya', *Studies in Third World Societies*, 8 (1979), pp. 37-56

Johnson, Steven L., 'Production, exchange, and economic development among the Luo-Abasuba of southwestern Kenya', PhD dissertation, Indiana University, 1980

Karani, Florida, 'The history of Maseno School, 1906-1962, its alumni and the local society', MA thesis, Nairobi University, 1974

Kenny, Michael G., 'Salt trading in eastern Lake Victoria', *Azania*, 9 (1975), pp. 225-8

Kenny, Michael G., 'The relation of oral history to social structure in South Nyanza, Kenya', *Africa*, 47, 3 (1977), pp. 276-88

Kenny, Michael G., 'Pre-colonial trade in eastern Lake Victoria', *Azania*, 14 (1979), pp. 97-107

Kenyatta, Jomo, *Facing Mount Kenya* (London, Secker and Warburg, 1953)

Kitching, Gavin, *Class and Economic Change in Kenya: The Making of an African Petite-Bourgeoisie* (New Haven, Yale University Press, 1980)

Kokwaro, J. O., 'Traditional medicine as one of the oldest African sciences', UNESCO Seminar on Oral Tradition, Past Growth and Future Development in East Africa, Kisumu, 1979

Lonsdale, John, 'A political history of Nyanza: 1883-1945', PhD dissertation, Cambridge University, 1946

Lonsdale, John, 'When did the Gusii (or any other group) become a tribe?', *Kenya Historical Review*, 5, 1 (1977), pp. 123-33

Macgoye, Marjorie Oludhe, *Coming to Birth* (Nairobi, Heinemann, 1986)

Malo, Shadrack, *Dhoudi Mag Central Nyanza* (Nairobi, Eagle Press, 1953)

Malo, Shadrack, *Dhoudi Moko Mag Luo* (Kisumu, Oluoch Publishing House, 1981) (a reprint of *Dhoudi Mag Central Nyanza*)

Mboya, Paul, *Luo Kitgi gi Timbegi* (Nairobi, Equatorial Publishers, 1938)

Medick, Hans, 'Missionare im Ruderboot? Ethnologische Erkenntnisweisen als Heransforderung an die Sozialgeschichte', *Geschichte und Gesellschaft*, 10, 3 (1984), pp. 295-319

Munro, J. Forbes, *Colonial Rule and the Kamba: Social Change in the Kenya Highlands, 1889-1939* (Oxford, Clarendon Press, 1975)

Mwangi, Meja, *Going Down River Road* (London, Heinemann, 1976)

Ndisi, John W., *A Study in the Economic and Social Life of the Luo of Kenya* (Lund, Berlingska Boktryckeriet, 1974)

New, Charles, *Life, Wanderings, and Labours in Eastern Africa* (London, Hodder, 1873)

Ng'anga, James Mwangi, *Kenya: A Subject Index. A Select Bibliography of Articles, 1967-1976* (Nairobi, African Book Services, 1983)

Ochieng', William R., 'Clan settlement and clan conflict in the Yimbo Location of Nyanza, 1500-1915', in B. G. McIntosh (ed.), *Ngano: Nairobi Historical Studies, I* (Nairobi, East African Publishing House, 1969), pp. 48-71

Ochieng', William R., 'Colonial African chiefs: were they primarily self-seeking scoundrels?', in B. A. Ogot (ed.), *Politics and Nationalism in Colonial Kenya* (Nairobi, East African Publishing House, 1972), pp. 46-70

Ochieng', William R., *An Outline History of Nyanza up to 1914* (Nairobi, East African Literature Bureau, 1974)

Ochieng', William R., 'Political and structural continuity in Yimbo, c. 1700-1972, in William R. Ochieng', *The First Word: Essays on Kenya History* (Nairobi, East African Literature Bureau, 1975), pp.130-156

Ochieng', William R., *A History of the Kadimo Chiefdom of Yimbo in Western Kenya* (Nairobi, East African Literature Bureau, 1975)

Ochieng', William R., 'The transformation of a Bantu settlement into a Luo Ruothdom: a case study of the evolution of the Yimbo community in Nyanza up to A.D. 1900', in B.A. Ogot (ed.), *Hadith 6; History and Social Change in East Africa* (Nairobi, East African Literature Bureau, 1976), pp. 44-64

Ocholla-Ayayo, A. B. C., *Traditional Ideology and Ethics among the Southern Luo* (Uppsala, Scandanavian Institute of African Studies, 1976)

Ocholla-Ayayo, A. B. C., 'Marriage and cattle exchange among the Nilotic Luo', *Paideuma*, 25 (1979), pp. 173-93

Ocholla-Ayayo, A. B. C., *The Luo Culture: A Reconstruction of the Material Culture Patterns of a Traditional African Society* (Weisbaden, Franz Steiner Verlag, 1980)

Odaga, Asenath B., 'Some aspects of the Luo traditional education transmitted through the oral narratives: *sigendini*', UNESCO Seminar on Oral Traditions, Past Growth and Future Development in East Africa, Kisumu, 1979

Odhiambo, E. S. Atieno, 'Some aspects of religious activity among the Uyoma fisherman: the rites connected with the launching of a fishing vessel', *Mila*, 1, 2 (1970), pp. 14-21

Odhiambo, E. S. Atieno, 'The rise and fall of the Kenya peasant, 1888-1922', in Peter C. W. Gutkind and Peter Waterman (eds), *African Social Studies: A Radical Reader* (London, Heinemann,

1977). Originally published in *East African Journal*, 9, 5 (1972), pp. 5-11

Odhiambo, E. S. Atieno, 'A portrait of Protestant missionaries in Kenya before 1939', in E. S. Atieno Odhiambo, *The Paradox of Collaboration and Other Essays* (Nairobi, East African Literature Bureau, 1974)

Odhiambo, E. S. Atieno, '"Seek ye first the Economic Kingdom". A history of the Luo Thrift and Trading Corporation (LUTATCO), 1945-56', in B. A. Ogot (ed.), *Hadith 5: Economic and Social History of East Africa* (Nairobi, East African Literature Bureau, 1975),pp. 218-56

Odhiambo, E. S. Atieno, 'Economic mobilization and political leadership: Oginga Odinga and the Luo Thrift and Trading Corporation to 1956', in Aloo Ojuka and William Ochieng' (eds), *Politics and Leadership in Africa* (Nairobi, East African Literature Bureau, 1975)

Odhiambo, E. S. Atieno, 'The movement of ideas: a case study of intellectual responses to colonialism among the Liganua peasants', in B. A. Ogot (ed.), *History and Social Change in East Africa* (Nairobi, East African Literature Bureau, 1976).

Odhiambo, E. S. Atieno, 'Siasa: African politics and nationalism in East Africa, 1919-1935', in E. S. Atieno Odhiambo, *Siasa: Politics and Nationalism in East Africa 1905-1939* (Nairobi, Kenya Literature Bureau. 1981), pp. 91-148

Odhiambo, E. S. Atieno, 'Towards a history of African traditional religion: a West Kenya case', unpublished paper

Odhiambo, O. J. H., 'Dholuo phonology: a study of the major vowel processes', MA dissertation, Nairobi, 1981

Odinga, Oginga, *Not yet Uhuru: An Autobiography* (New York, Hill & Wang, 1969)

Odongo, Onyango Ku, and J. B. Webster (eds), *The Central Lwo during the Aconya* (Nairobi, East African Literature Bureau, 1976)

Ogot, B. A., 'British administration in the Central Nyanza District of Kenya', *Journal of African History*, 4, 2 (1963), pp.249-73

Ogot, B. A., 'Kingship and statelessness among the Nilotes', in Jan Vansina, R. Mauny, and L. V. Thomas (eds), *The Historian in Tropical Africa* (London, Oxford University Press, 1964), pp. 284-302

Ogot, B. A., *History of the Southern Luo: Migration and Settlement* (Nairobi, East African Publishing House, 1967)

Ogot, B. A., and William R. Ochieng', 'Mumboism; an anti-colonial movement', in B. A. Ogot (ed.), *War and Society in Africa* (London, Frank Cass, 1972), pp. 149-77

Ogot, Grace, *The Promised Land* (Nairobi, East African Publishing House, 1966)

Ogutu, G. E. M., 'A case for oral traditions in the study of belief systems and ritual', UNESCO Seminar on Oral Traditions, Past Growth and Future Development in East Africa, Kisumu, 1979

Ogutu-Obunga, G. E. M., 'The ideas of time and history with special reference to the Kenya Luo', *Kenya Historical Review*, 2, 1 (1974), pp.13-21

Okaro-Kojwang, K. M., 'Origins and establishment of the Kavirondo Taxpayers' Welfare Association', in B. C. McIntosh (ed.), *Ngano: Nairobi Historical Studies, I* (Nairobi, East African Publishing House, 1969)

Okot p'Bitek, *Religion of the Central Luo* (Nairobi, Kenya Literature Bureau, 1971)

Okoth-Okombo, Duncan, *Dholuo Morphophonemics in a Generative Framework* (Berlin, Dietrich Reimer Verlag, 1982)

Oliver, Roland, 'The Nilotic contribution to Bantu Africa', in Rainer Vossen and Marianne Bechhaus-Gerst (eds), *Nilotic Studies: Proceedings of the International Symposium on Languages and History of the Nilotic peoples, Cologne, January 4-6, 1982* (Berlin, Dietrich Reimer Verlag, 1983), Vol.2, pp.357-74

Oloo (Aringo), Peter C., 'History of settlement: the example of Luo clans of Alego (1500-1918)', BA dissertation, University of East Africa (University College, Nairobi), 1969

Ominde, Simeon H., *The Luo Girl from Infancy to Marriage* (Nairobi, East African Literature Bureau, 1952)

Omondi, Lucia Ndong'a, *The Major Syntactic Structures of Dholuo* (Berlin, Dietrich Reimer Verlag, 1982)

Onyango-Ogutu, B., and A. A. Roscoe, *Keep My Words: Luo Oral Literature* (Nairobi, East African Publishing House, 1974)

Otieno, Margaret, 'The biography of ex-Chief Muganda Okwako (1903-1952)', BA dissertation, Nairobi, 1972

Parkin, David, *The Cultural Definition of Political Response: Lineal Destiny among the Luo* (London, Academic Press, 1978)

Potash, Betty, 'Marriage stability in a rural Luo community', *Africa*, 48, 4 (1978), pp. 381-97

Ranger, T. O., *Dance and Society in Eastern Africa, 1890-1970: The Beni Ngoma* (London, Heinemann, 1975)

Schiller, Lawrence D., 'Gem and Kano: a comparative study of stress in two traditional African political systems in Nyanza Province, Western Kenya, c.1850-1914', paper presented to the Nairobi History Seminar, 1977

Shipton, Parker M., 'Lineage and locality as antithetical principles in East African systems of land tenure', *Ethnology*, 23, 2 (1984), pp. 117-32

Shipton, Parker M., 'Strips and patches: a demographic dimension in some African land-holding and political systems', *Man*, 19 (1984), pp 613-34

Southall, Aidan, *Lineage Formation among the Luo* (London, Oxford University Press, 1952)

Southall, Aidan, *Alur Society. A Study in Processes and Types of Domination* (Cambridge, Heffer, 1956)

Southall, Aidan, 'Rank and stratification among the Alur and other Nilotic peoples', in Arthur Tuden and Leonard Plotnicov (eds), *Social Stratification in Africa* (New York, Free Press, 1970), pp. 31-46

Southall, Aidan, 'From segmentary lineage to ethnic association: Luo, Luyia, Ibo, and others', in M. Owusu (ed.), *Colonialism and Change: Essays Presented to Lucy Mair* (The Hague, Mouton, 1975)

Spittler, Gerd, 'Administration in a peasant state', *Sociologia Ruralis*, 23 (1980), pp. 130-44

Stafford, R. l., *An Elementary Luo Grammar, with Vocabularies* (Nairobi, Oxford University Press, 1967)

Tosh, John, 'Lango agriculture during the early colonial period: land and labour in a cash-crop economy', *Journal of African History*, 19, 3 (1978), pp.415-439

Tucker, A. N., and M. A. Bryan, *Linguistic Analyses. The Non-Bantu Languages of North-Eastern Africa* (London, Oxford University Press, 1952)

Vansina, Jan, *Oral Tradition* (London, Routledge & Kegan Paul, 1965)

Vansina, Jan, *Oral Tradition as History* (Madison, University of Wisconsin Press; London, James Currey & Nairobi, Heinemann Kenya, 1985)

Were, Priscilla O., 'The origin and growth of the iron industry and trade in Samia (Kenya)', BA dissertation, University College, Nairobi, 1972

Whisson, Michael, 'Some aspects of functional disorders among the Kenya Luo', in Ari Kiev (ed.), *Magic, Faith and Healing: Studies in Primitive Psychiatry Today* (New York, Free Press, 1964), pp. 283-304

Whisson, Michael, *Change and Challenge: A Study of the Social and Economic Changes among the Kenya Luo* (Nairobi, Christian Council of Kenya, 1964)

Whisson, Michael, and John Lonsdale, 'The case of Jason Gor and fourteen others: a succession dispute in historical perspective', *Africa*, 45, 1, (1976) pp. 50-65

Wilks, Ivor, 'Land, labour and the forest kingdom of Asante', in J. Friedman and M. J. Rowlands (eds), *The Evolution of Social Systems* (Pittsburgh, University of Pittsburgh Press, 1977), pp 487-534

Wilson, Gordon, *Luo Customary Law and Marriage Customs* (Nairobi, Government Printer, 1968)

Zwanenberg, R. M. van, 'The missionary conscience and colonial injustices: the life and times of W. E. Owen of Nyanza', in Aloo Ojuka and William Ochieng' (eds), *Politics and Leadership in Africa* (Nairobi, East African Literature Bureau, 1975), pp. 63-84

Index

Siaya

taxes, 10, 73-74, 76

ugali, 45-46, 65. See also maize, food
Uganda, 18-21, 36, 79; Luo settlers in, 47-50;
    smuggling across border with Kenya,
    51-53
Ugenya, ii, 36; 'Riviera', 50

Vansina, Jan, 30, 41 n
Voice of Kenya, 119, 134-35
voluntary associations, 33-35, 43-45, 87-88

wat. See kinship
Wilks, Ivor, 13, 22 n
women, 129-30; aesthetics and, 114; and
    'runaway husbands', 49-50; and birthing, 25;
    and Christianity, 95-96, 115-16; and hunger,
    61-67; and male discourse, 85-86; and
    therapy, 6; as household heads, 87-88; begg-
    ing, 67

Yimbo, 28-29, 103-09, 110 n
youth, 96-99, 117-19